Great Battles of World War Two

Battle of Berlin

Compiled by

Edith Cothran

Scribbles

Year of Publication 2018

ISBN : 9789352979356

Book Published by

Scribbles

(An Imprint of Alpha Editions)

email - alphaedis@gmail.com

Produced by: PediaPress GmbH
Limburg an der Lahn
Germany
http://pediapress.com/

Contents

Introduction

Battle of Berlin

<indicator name="pp-default"> 🔒 </indicator>

Battle of Berlin	
Part of the Eastern Front of World War II	

The Brandenburg Gate amid the ruins of Berlin, June 1945

Date	16 April – 2 May 1945
Location	Berlin, Germany 52°31′N 13°23′E[1] Coordinates: 52°31′N 13°23′E[1]
Result	Decisive Soviet victory • Suicide of Adolf Hitler and deaths of other high-ranking Nazi officials • Unconditional surrender of the Berlin city garrison on 2 May. • Capitulation of German forces still fighting the battle outside Berlin on 8/9 May, following the unconditional surrender of all German forces • End of World War II in Europe and the destruction of Nazi Germany
Territorial changes	Soviets occupy what would become East Germany during the Partition of Germany later that year.
Belligerents	
• ▇▇▇ Soviet Union • ▨▨ Poland	🅂 Germany
Commanders and leaders	

• ▮▮▮	• ⚑
• 1st Belorussian Front:	• Army Group Vistula:
• Georgy Zhukov	• Gotthard Heinrici
2nd Belorussian Front:	• Kurt von Tippelskirch ⚑
• Konstantin Rokossovsky	Army Group Centre:
1st Ukrainian Front:	• Ferdinand Schörner
• Ivan Konev	Berlin Defence Area:
	• Hellmuth Reymann
	• Helmuth Weidling ⚑

Strength	
• Total strength:	• Total strength:
• 2,500,000 soldiers (155,900 –	• 36 divisions[7]
c.200,000 Polish People's Army)[2,3]	• 766,750 soldiers[8]
• 6,250 tanks and SP guns[3]	• 1,519 AFVs[9]
• 7,500 aircraft[3]	• 2,224 aircraft[10]
• 41,600 artillery pieces.[4,5]	• 9,303 artillery pieces[8]
• For the investment and assault on the	• In the Berlin Defence Area: about
Berlin Defence Area: about 1,500,000	45,000 soldiers, supplemented by the
soldiers[6]	police force, Hitler Youth, and 40,000
	Volkssturm[6]

Casualties and losses	
• Archival research	• Estimated:
(operational total)	92,000–100,000 killed
• 81,116 dead or missing[11]	• 220,000 wounded[13]
• 280,251 sick or wounded	• 480,000 captured[14]
• 1,997 tanks and SPGs destroyed[12]	• Inside Berlin Defence Area:
• 2,108 artillery pieces	• about 22,000 military dead
• 917 aircraft[12]	• 22,000 civilian dead[15]

Part of a series on the
History of Berlin

Margraviate of Brandenburg (1157–1806)
Kingdom of Prussia (1701–1918)
German Empire (1871–1918)
Weimar Republic (1919–1933)
• 1920s Berlin • Greater Berlin Act
Nazi Germany (1933–1945)
• Welthauptstadt Germania • Bombing of Berlin in World War II • Battle of Berlin

West Germany and East Germany (1945–1990)		
• West Berlin and East Berlin		
• Berlin Wall		
• Berlin Blockade (1948–1949)		
• Berlin Crisis of 1961		
• "Ich bin ein Berliner" (1963)		
• "Tear Down This Wall" (1987)		
Federal Republic of Germany (1990–present)		
• History of Germany and History of Europe		
See also		
• Timeline of Berlin		
• <u>v</u> • <u>t</u> • <u>e</u>[16]		

The **Battle of Berlin**, designated the **Berlin Strategic Offensive Operation** by the Soviet Union, and also known as the **Fall of Berlin**, was the final major offensive of the European theatre of World War II.

Following the Vistula–Oder Offensive of January–February 1945, the Red Army had temporarily halted on a line 60 km (37 mi) east of Berlin. On 9 March, Germany established its defence plan for the city with Operation Clausewitz. The first defensive preparations at the outskirts of Berlin were made on 20 March, under the newly appointed commander of Army Group Vistula, General Gotthard Heinrici.

When the Soviet offensive resumed on 16 April, two Soviet fronts (army groups) attacked Berlin from the east and south, while a third overran German forces positioned north of Berlin. Before the main battle in Berlin commenced, the Red Army encircled the city after successful battles of the Seelow Heights and Halbe. On 20 April 1945, Hitler's birthday, the 1st Belorussian Front led by Marshal Georgy Zhukov, advancing from the east and north, started shelling Berlin's city centre, while Marshal Ivan Konev's 1st Ukrainian Front broke through Army Group Centre and advanced towards the southern sub-urbs of Berlin. On 23 April General Helmuth Weidling assumed command of the forces within Berlin. The garrison consisted of several depleted and disorganised Wehrmacht and Waffen-SS divisions, along with poorly trained *Volkssturm* and Hitler Youth members. Over the course of the next week, the Red Army gradually took the entire city.

Before the battle was over, Hitler and several of his followers killed themselves. The city's garrison surrendered on 2 May but fighting continued to the north-west, west, and south-west of the city until the end of the war in Europe on 8

Figure 1: *Main thrusts of the Red Army and its eastern allies.*

May (9 May in the Soviet Union) as some German units fought westward so that they could surrender to the Western Allies rather than to the Soviets.[17]

Background

Starting on 12 January 1945, the Red Army began the Vistula–Oder Offensive across the Narew River; and, from Warsaw, a three-day operation on a broad front, which incorporated four army Fronts.[18] On the fourth day, the Red Army broke out and started moving west, up to 30 to 40 km (19 to 25 mi) per day, taking East Prussia, Danzig, and Poznań, drawing up on a line 60 km (37 mi) east of Berlin along the Oder River.[19]

The newly created Army Group Vistula, under the command of *Reichsführer-SS* Heinrich Himmler,[20] attempted a counter-attack, but this had failed by 24 February.[21] The Red Army then drove on to Pomerania, clearing the right bank of the Oder River, thereby reaching into Silesia.[19]

In the south the Siege of Budapest raged. Three German divisions attempts to relieve the encircled Hungarian capital city failed, and Budapest fell to the Soviets on 13 February.[22] Adolf Hitler insisted on a counter-attack to recapture the Drau-Danube triangle.[23] The goal was to secure the oil region of

Neustrelitz
3 Pz Army O Prenzlau
Pritzwalk Wittstock/Dosse
Army Group
of gen. Steiner
11 Army
Schwedt
2nd Belorussian Front
Wittenberge Gransee Angermunde
Havelberg Neuruppin
Gorzów Wlkp. Krzyż
1 Army Eberswalde
Nauen Bernau Kostrzyń Warta
Stendal
Strausberg
Ketzin 1st Belorussian Front
Potsdam Frankfurt on the Oder
12 Army Mittenwalde Fürstenberg Zbąszyń
Magdeburg Luckenwalde 9 Beeskow Army
Krosno Odrzańskie
Lutherstadt Wittenberg Lübben Gubin Zielona Góra Oder (Odra)
Cottbus Forst (Lausitz) Bad Muskau
Halle (Saale) Torgau Głogów
Leipzig 1st Ukrainian Front
Panzer Group 2 Army Rothenburg
Army Group Centre Zgorzelec
of gen. Schörner Kamenz Görlitz
Erfurt Dresden Bautzen Luban Lusatian Neisse (Nysa Łużycka)
4 Pz Army 17 Army

Battle of Berlin
German attempts to relieve Berlin (April - May 1945)
- - - - Position of Polish forces
- - - - Position of Soviet forces
- - - - Position of German forces
Direction of German retreat
Direction of German offensive

Figure 2: *German counter-attacks.*

Nagykanizsa and regain the Danube River for future operations,[24] but the depleted German forces had been given an impossible task.[25] By 16 March, the German Lake Balaton Offensive had failed, and a counter-attack by the Red Army took back in 24 hours everything the Germans had taken ten days to gain.[26] On 30 March, the Soviets entered Austria; and in the Vienna Offensive they captured Vienna on 13 April.[27]

Between June and September 1944, the Wehrmacht had lost more than a million men, and it lacked the fuel and armaments needed to operate effectively.[28] On 12 April 1945, Hitler, who had earlier decided to remain in the city against the wishes of his advisers, heard the news that the American President Franklin D. Roosevelt had died.[29] This briefly raised false hopes in the *Führerbunker* that there might yet be a falling out among the Allies and that Berlin would be saved at the last moment, as had happened once before when Berlin was threatened (see the Miracle of the House of Brandenburg).[30]

No plans were made by the Western Allies to seize the city by a ground operation.[31] The Supreme Commander [Western] Allied Expeditionary Force, General Eisenhower lost interest in the race to Berlin and saw no further need to suffer casualties by attacking a city that would be in the Soviet sphere of influence after the war,[32] envisioning excessive friendly fire if both armies attempted to occupy the city at once.[33] The major Western Allied contribution to the battle was the bombing of Berlin during 1945.[34] During 1945 the United States Army Air Forces launched very large daytime raids on Berlin and for 36 nights in succession, scores of RAF Mosquitos bombed the German capital, ending on the night of 20/21 April 1945 just before the Soviets entered the city.[35]

Preparations

The Soviet offensive into central Germany, what later became East Germany, had two objectives. Stalin did not believe the Western Allies would hand over territory occupied by them in the post-war Soviet zone, so he began the offensive on a broad front and moved rapidly to meet the Western Allies as far west as possible. But the overriding objective was to capture Berlin.[36] The two goals were complementary because possession of the zone could not be won quickly unless Berlin were taken. Another consideration was that Berlin itself held useful post-war strategic assets, including Adolf Hitler and the German atomic bomb programme.[37] On 6 March, Hitler appointed Lieutenant General Helmuth Reymann commander of the Berlin Defence Area, replacing Lieutenant General Bruno Ritter von Hauenschild.[38]

On 20 March, General Gotthard Heinrici was appointed Commander-in-Chief of Army Group Vistula replacing *Reichsführer-SS* Heinrich Himmler.[39] Heinrici was one of the best defensive tacticians in the German army, and he immediately started to lay defensive plans. Heinrici correctly assessed that the main Soviet thrust would be made over the Oder River and along the main east-west Autobahn.[40] He decided not to try to defend the banks of the Oder with anything more than a light skirmishing screen. Instead, Heinrici arranged for engineers to fortify the Seelow Heights, which overlooked the Oder River at the point where the Autobahn crossed them.[41] This was some distance 17 km (11 mi) west of the Oder and 90 km (56 mi) east of Berlin. Heinrici thinned out the line in other areas to increase the manpower available to defend the heights. German engineers turned the Oder's flood plain, already saturated by the spring thaw, into a swamp by releasing the water from a reservoir upstream. Behind the plain on the plateau, the engineers built three belts of defensive emplacements[41] reaching back towards the outskirts of Berlin (the lines nearer to Berlin were called the *Wotan* position).[42] These lines consisted of anti-tank ditches, anti-tank gun emplacements, and an extensive network of trenches and bunkers.[41,42]

On 9 April, after a long resistance, Königsberg in East Prussia fell to the Red Army. This freed up Marshal Rokossovsky's 2nd Belorussian Front to move west to the east bank of the Oder river.[43] Marshal Georgy Zhukov concentrated his 1st Belorussian Front, which had been deployed along the Oder river from Frankfurt in the south to the Baltic, into an area in front of the Seelow Heights.[44] The 2nd Belorussian Front moved into the positions being vacated by the 1st Belorussian Front north of the Seelow Heights. While this redeployment was in progress, gaps were left in the lines; and the remnants of General Dietrich von Saucken's German II Army, which had been bottled up in a pocket near Danzig, managed to escape into the Vistula Delta.[45] To the south, Marshal Konev shifted the main weight of the 1st Ukrainian Front out of Upper Silesia and north-west to the Neisse River.[4]

The three Soviet fronts had altogether 2.5 million men (including 78,556 soldiers of the 1st Polish Army), 6,250 tanks, 7,500 aircraft, 41,600 artillery pieces and mortars, 3,255 truck-mounted Katyusha rocket launchers (nicknamed 'Stalin's Pipe Organs'), and 95,383 motor vehicles, many manufactured in the US.[4]

Battle of the Oder–Neisse

The sector in which most of the fighting in the overall offensive took place was the Seelow Heights, the last major defensive line outside Berlin.[42] The Battle of the Seelow Heights, fought over four days from 16 April until 19 April, was one of the last pitched battles of World War II: almost one million Red Army soldiers and more than 20,000 tanks and artillery pieces were deployed to break through the "Gates to Berlin", which were defended by about 100,000 German soldiers and 1,200 tanks and guns.[46,47] The Soviet forces led by Zhukov broke through the defensive positions, having suffered about 30,000 dead,[48,49] while 12,000 German personnel were killed.[49]

During 19 April, the fourth day, the 1st Belorussian Front broke through the final line of the Seelow Heights; and nothing but broken German formations lay between them and Berlin.[50] The 1st Ukrainian Front, having captured Forst the day before, was fanning out into open country.[51] One powerful thrust by Gordov's 3rd Guards Army and Rybalko's 3rd and Lelyushenko's 4th Guards Tank Armies were heading north-east towards Berlin while other armies headed west towards a section of the United States Army's front line south-west of Berlin on the Elbe.[52] With these advances, the Soviet forces drove a wedge between the German Army Group Vistula in the north and Army Group Centre in the south.[52] By the end of the day, the German eastern front line north of Frankfurt around Seelow and to the south around Forst had ceased to exist. These breakthroughs allowed the two Soviet Fronts to envelop the German 9th Army in a large pocket west of Frankfurt. Attempts by the 9th Army to break out to the west resulted in the Battle of Halbe.[47] The cost to the Soviet forces had been very high, with over 2,807 tanks lost between 1 and 19 April, including at least 727 at the Seelow Heights.[53]

Figure 3: *March 1945: Photo of 16-year-old Willi Hübner being awarded the Iron Cross II Class medal for his defense of Lauban.*

In the meantime, RAF Mosquitos were conducting large tactical air raids against German positions inside Berlin on the nights of 15 April (105 bombers), 17 April (61 bombers), 18 April (57 bombers), 19 April (79 bombers), and 20 April (78 bombers).[54]

Encirclement of Berlin

On 20 April 1945, Hitler's 56th birthday, Soviet artillery of the 1st Belorussian Front began shelling Berlin and did not stop until the city surrendered. The weight of ordnance delivered by Soviet artillery during the battle was greater than the total tonnage dropped by Western Allied bombers on the city.[55] While the 1st Belorussian Front advanced towards the east and north-east of the city, the 1st Ukrainian Front pushed through the last formations of the northern wing of Army Group Centre and passed north of Juterbog, well over halfway to the American front line on the river Elbe at Magdeburg.[56] To the north between Stettin and Schwedt, the 2nd Belorussian Front attacked the northern flank of Army Group Vistula, held by Hasso von Manteuffel's III Panzer Army.[53] The next day, Bogdanov's 2nd Guards Tank Army advanced nearly 50 km (31 mi) north of Berlin and then attacked south-west of Werneuchen. The Soviet plan was to encircle Berlin first and then envelop the IX Army.[57]

Figure 4: *April 1945: a member of the Volkssturm, the German home defence militia, armed with Panzerschreck, outside Berlin.*

The command of the German V Corps, trapped with the IX Army north of Forst, passed from the IV Panzer Army to the IX Army. The corps was still holding on to the Berlin-Cottbus highway front line.[58] Field Marshal Ferdinand Schörner's Army Group Centre launched a counter-offensive aimed at breaking through to Berlin from the south and making a successful initial incursion (the Battle of Bautzen) in the 1st Ukrainian Front region, engaging the 2nd Polish Army and elements of the Red Army's 52nd Army and 5th Guards Army.[59] When the old southern flank of the IV Panzer Army had some local successes counter-attacking north against the 1st Ukrainian Front, Hitler gave orders that showed his grasp of military reality was completely gone. He ordered the IX Army to hold Cottbus and set up a front facing west.[60] Then they were to attack the Soviet columns advancing north. This would supposedly allow them to form a northern pincer that would meet the IV Panzer Army coming from the south and envelop the 1st Ukrainian Front before destroying it.[61] They were to anticipate a southward attack by the III Panzer Army and be ready to be the southern arm of a pincer attack that would envelop 1st Belorussian Front, which would be destroyed by SS-General Felix Steiner's Army Detachment advancing from north of Berlin.[62] Later in the day, when Steiner explained that he did not have the divisions to do this, Heinrici made it clear to Hitler's staff that unless the IX Army retreated immediately, it would be enveloped by the Soviets. He stressed that it was already too late for it to move north-west to Berlin and would have to retreat west.[62] Heinrici went on to say that if Hitler did not allow it to move west, he would ask to be relieved of his command.[63]

On 22 April 1945, at his afternoon situation conference, Hitler fell into a tearful rage (famously dramatized in the 2004 German film *Downfall*) when he realised that his plans, prepared the previous day, could not be achieved. He declared that the war was lost, blaming the generals for the defeat and that he would remain in Berlin until the end and then kill himself.[64]

In an attempt to coax Hitler out of his rage, General Alfred Jodl speculated that General Walther Wenck's XII Army, which was facing the Americans, could move to Berlin because the Americans, already on the Elbe River, were unlikely to move further east. This assumption was based on his viewing of the captured Eclipse documents, which organised the partition of Germany among the Allies.[65] Hitler immediately grasped the idea, and within hours Wenck was ordered to disengage from the Americans and move the XII Army north-east to support Berlin.[62] It was then realised that if the IX Army moved west, it could link up with the XII Army. In the evening Heinrici was given permission to make the link-up.[66]

Elsewhere, the 2nd Belorussian Front had established a bridgehead 15 km (9 mi) deep on the west bank of the Oder and was heavily engaged with the III Panzer Army.[67] The IX Army had lost Cottbus and was being pressed from the east. A Soviet tank spearhead was on the Havel River to the east of Berlin, and another had at one point penetrated the inner defensive ring of Berlin.[68]

The capital was now within range of field artillery. A Soviet war correspondent, in the style of World War II Soviet journalism, gave the following account of an important event which took place on 22 April 1945 at 08:30 local time:[69]

On the walls of the houses we saw Goebbels' appeals, hurriedly scrawled in white paint: 'Every German will defend his capital. We shall stop the Red hordes at the walls of our Berlin.' Just try and stop them!
Steel pillboxes, barricades, mines, traps, suicide squads with grenades clutched in their hands—all are swept aside before the tidal wave.
Drizzling rain began to fall. Near Bisdorf I saw batteries preparing to open fire.
'What are the targets?' I asked the battery commander.
'Centre of Berlin, Spree bridges, and the northern and Stettin railway stations,' he answered.
Then came the tremendous words of command: 'Open fire on the capital of Fascist Germany.'
I noted the time. It was exactly 8:30 a.m. on 22 April. Ninety-six shells fell in the centre of Berlin in the course of a few minutes.

On 23 April 1945, the Soviet 1st Belorussian Front and 1st Ukrainian Front continued to tighten the encirclement, severing the last link between the German IX Army and the city.[68] Elements of the 1st Ukrainian Front continued to move westward and started to engage the German XII Army moving towards Berlin. On this same day, Hitler appointed General Helmuth Weidling as the commander of the Berlin Defence Area, replacing Lieutenant General Reymann.[70] Meanwhile, by 24 April 1945 elements of 1st Belorussian Front and 1st Ukrainian Front had completed the encirclement of the city.[71] Within the next day, 25 April 1945, the Soviet investment of Berlin was consolidated, with leading Soviet units probing and penetrating the S-Bahn defensive ring.[72] By the end of the day, it was clear that the German defence of the city could not do anything but temporarily delay the capture of the city by the Soviets, since the decisive stages of the battle had already been fought and lost by the Germans outside the city.[73] By that time, Schörner's offensive, initially successful, had mostly been thwarted, although he did manage to inflict significant casualties on the opposing Polish and Soviet units, slowing down their progress.[59]

Battle in Berlin

The forces available to General Weidling for the city's defence included roughly 45,000 soldiers in several severely depleted German Army and Waffen-SS divisions.[6] These divisions were supplemented by the police force, boys in the compulsory Hitler Youth, and the *Volkssturm*.[6] Many of the 40,000 elderly men of the *Volkssturm* had been in the army as young men and some were veterans of World War I. Hitler appointed *SS Brigadeführer* Wilhelm Mohnke the Battle Commander for the central government district that included the Reich Chancellery and *Führerbunker*.[74] He had over 2,000 men under his command.[6] Weidling organised the defences into eight sectors designated 'A' through to 'H' each one commanded by a colonel or a general, but most had no combat experience.[6] To the west of the city was the 20th Infantry Division. To the north of the city was the 9th Parachute Division.[75] To the north-east of the city was the Panzer Division *Müncheberg*. To the south-east of the city and to the east of Tempelhof Airport was the 11th SS Panzergrenadier Division *Nordland*.[76] The reserve, 18th Panzergrenadier Division, was in Berlin's central district.[77]

On 23 April, Berzarin's 5th Shock Army and Katukov's 1st Guards Tank Army assaulted Berlin from the south-east and, after overcoming a counter-attack by the German LVI Panzer Corps, reached the Berlin S-Bahn ring railway on the north side of the Teltow Canal by the evening of 24 April.[52] During the same period, of all the German forces ordered to reinforce the inner defences of the city by Hitler, only a small contingent of French SS volunteers under the command of *SS Brigadeführer* Gustav Krukenberg arrived in Berlin.[78] During 25 April, Krukenberg was appointed as the commander of Defence Sector C, the sector under the most pressure from the Soviet assault on the city.[79]

On 26 April, Chuikov's 8th Guards Army and the 1st Guards Tank Army fought their way through the southern suburbs and attacked Tempelhof Airport, just inside the S-Bahn defensive ring, where they met stiff resistance from the *Müncheberg* Division.[78] But by 27 April, the two understrength divisions (*Müncheberg* and *Nordland*) that were defending the south-east, now facing five Soviet armies—from east to west, the 5th Shock Army, the 8th Guards Army, the 1st Guards Tank Army and Rybalko's 3rd Guards Tank Army (part of the 1st Ukrainian Front)—were forced back towards the centre, taking up new defensive positions around Hermannplatz.[80] Krukenberg informed General Hans Krebs, Chief of the General Staff of (OKH) that within 24 hours the *Nordland* would have to fall back to the centre sector Z (for *Zentrum*).[81,82] The Soviet advance to the city centre was along these main axes: from the southeast, along the Frankfurter Allee (ending and stopped at the Alexanderplatz); from the south along Sonnenallee ending north of the Belle-Alliance-Platz, from the south ending near the Potsdamer Platz and from the north ending near the Reichstag.[83] The Reichstag, the Moltke bridge, Alexanderplatz, and the Havel bridges at Spandau saw the heaviest fighting, with house-to-house and hand-to-hand combat. The foreign contingents of the SS fought particularly hard, because they were ideologically motivated and they believed that they would not live if captured.[84]

Battle for the Reichstag

In the early hours of 29 April the Soviet 3rd Shock Army crossed the Moltke bridge and started to fan out into the surrounding streets and buildings.[85] The initial assaults on buildings, including the Ministry of the Interior, were hampered by the lack of supporting artillery. It was not until the damaged bridges were repaired that artillery could be moved up in support.[86] At 04:00 hours, in the *Führerbunker*, Hitler signed his last will and testament and, shortly afterwards, married Eva Braun.[87] At dawn the Soviets pressed on with their assault in the south-east. After very heavy fighting they managed to capture Gestapo headquarters on Prinz-Albrechtstrasse, but a *Waffen-SS* counter-attack forced the Soviets to withdraw from the building.[88] To the south-west the 8th Guards Army attacked north across the Landwehr canal into the Tiergarten.[89]

By the next day, 30 April, the Soviets had solved their bridging problems and with artillery support at 06:00 they launched an attack on the Reichstag, but because of German entrenchments and support from 12.8 cm guns 2 km (1.2 mi) away on the roof of the Zoo flak tower, in Berlin Zoo, it was not

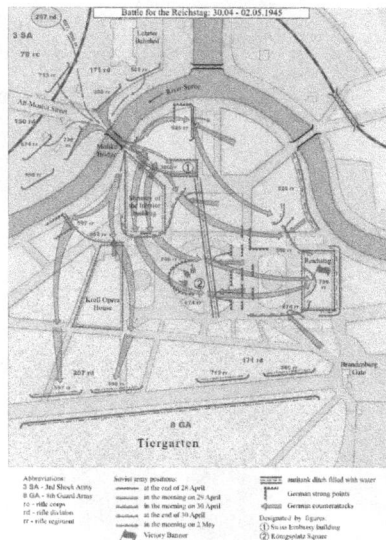

Figure 5: *Battle for the Reichstag.*

until that evening that the Soviets were able to enter the building.[90] The Reichstag had not been in use since it had burned in February 1933 and its interior resembled a rubble heap more than a government building. The German troops inside made excellent use of this and were heavily entrenched.[91] Fierce room-to-room fighting ensued. At that point there was still a large contingent of German soldiers in the basement who launched counter-attacks against the Red Army.[91] On 2 May 1945 the Red Army controlled the building entirely.[92] The famous photo of the two soldiers planting the flag on the roof of the building is a re-enactment photo taken the day after the building was taken.[93] To the Soviets the event as represented by the photo became symbolic of their victory demonstrating that the Battle of Berlin, as well as the Eastern Front hostilities as a whole, ended with the total Soviet victory.[94] As the 756th Regiment's commander Zinchenko had stated in his order to Battalion Commander Neustroev "... the Supreme High Command ... and the entire Soviet People order you to erect the victory banner on the roof above Berlin".[91]

Battle for the centre

During the early hours of 30 April, Weidling informed Hitler in person that the defenders would probably exhaust their ammunition during the night. Hitler gave him the permission to attempt a breakout through the encircling

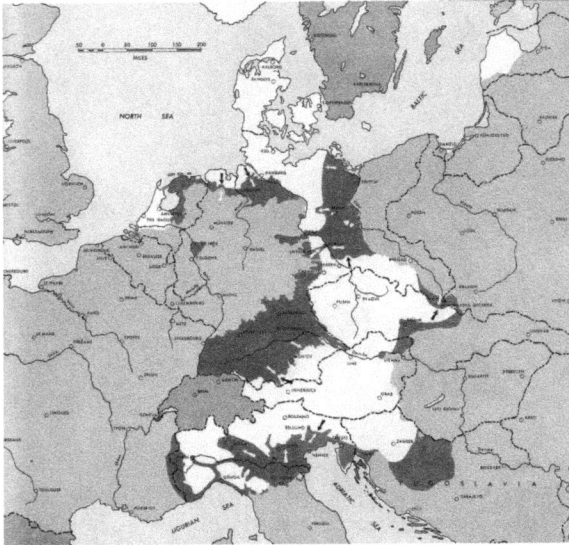

Figure 6: *Front lines 1 May (pink = allied occupied territory; red = area of fighting)*

Red Army lines.[95] That afternoon, Hitler and Braun committed suicide and
their bodies were cremated not far from the bunker.[96] In accordance with
Hitler's last will and testament, Admiral Karl Dönitz became the "President
of Germany" (*Reichspräsident*) in the new Flensburg government, and Joseph
Goebbels became the new Chancellor of Germany (*Reichskanzler*).[97]

As the perimeter shrank and the surviving defenders fell back, they became
concentrated into a small area in the city centre. By now there were about
10,000 German soldiers in the city centre, which was being assaulted from all
sides. One of the other main thrusts was along Wilhelmstrasse on which the
Air Ministry, built of reinforced concrete, was pounded by large concentrations of Soviet artillery.[90] The remaining German Tiger tanks of the Hermann
von Salza battalion took up positions in the east of the Tiergarten to defend
the centre against Kuznetsov's 3rd Shock Army (which although heavily engaged around the Reichstag was also flanking the area by advancing through
the northern Tiergarten) and the 8th Guards Army advancing through the south
of the Tiergarten.[98] These Soviet forces had effectively cut the sausage-shaped
area held by the Germans in half and made any escape attempt to the west for
German troops in the centre much more difficult.[99]

During the early hours of 1 May, Krebs talked to General Chuikov, commander of the Soviet 8th Guards Army,[100] informing him of Hitler's death and a willingness to negotiate a citywide surrender.[101] They could not agree on terms because of Soviet insistence on unconditional surrender and Krebs' claim that he lacked authorisation to agree to that.[102] Goebbels was against surrender. In the afternoon, Goebbels and his wife killed their children and then themselves.[103] Goebbels's death removed the last impediment which prevented Weidling from accepting the terms of unconditional surrender of his garrison, but he chose to delay the surrender until the next morning to allow the planned breakout to take place under the cover of darkness.[104]

Breakout and surrender

On the night of 1/2 May, most of the remnants of the Berlin garrison attempted to break out of the city centre in three different directions. Only those that went west through the Tiergarten and crossed the Charlottenbrücke (a bridge over the Havel) into Spandau succeeded in breaching Soviet lines.[105] Only a handful of those who survived the initial breakout made it to the lines of the Western Allies—most were either killed or captured by the Red Army's outer encirclement forces west of the city.[106] Early in the morning of 2 May, the Soviets captured the Reich Chancellery. General Weidling surrendered with his staff at 06:00 hours. He was taken to see General Vasily Chuikov at 08:23, where Weidling ordered the city's defenders to surrender to the Soviets.[107]

The 350-strong garrison of the Zoo flak tower left the building. There was sporadic fighting in a few isolated buildings where some SS troops still refused to surrender, but the Soviets reduced such buildings to rubble.[108]

Battle outside Berlin

At some point on 28 April or 29 April, General Gotthard Heinrici, Commander-in-Chief of Army Group Vistula, was relieved of his command after disobeying Hitler's direct orders to hold Berlin at all costs and never order a retreat, and was replaced by General Kurt Student.[109] General Kurt von Tippelskirch was named as Heinrici's interim replacement until Student could arrive and assume control. There remains some confusion as to who was in command, as some references say that Student was captured by the British and never arrived.[110] Regardless of whether von Tippelskirch or Student was in command of Army Group Vistula, the rapidly deteriorating situation that the Germans faced meant that Army Group Vistula's coordination of the armies under its nominal command during the last few days of the war was of little significance.[111]

On the evening of 29 April, Krebs contacted General Alfred Jodl (Supreme Army Command) by radio:[102]

> *Request immediate report. Firstly of the whereabouts of Wenck's spearheads. Secondly of time intended to attack. Thirdly of the location of the IX Army. Fourthly of the precise place in which the IX Army will break through. Fifthly of the whereabouts of General Rudolf Holste's spearhead.*

In the early morning of 30 April, Jodl replied to Krebs:[102]

> *Firstly, Wenck's spearhead bogged down south of Schwielow Lake. Secondly, the XII Army therefore unable to continue attack on Berlin. Thirdly, bulk of the IX Army surrounded. Fourthly, Holste's Corps on the defensive.*

North

While the 1st Belorussian Front and the 1st Ukrainian Front encircled Berlin, and started the battle for the city itself, Rokossovsky's 2nd Belorussian Front started his offensive to the north of Berlin. On 20 April between Stettin and Schwedt, Rokossovsky's 2nd Belorussian Front attacked the northern flank of Army Group Vistula, held by the III Panzer Army.[53] By 22 April, the 2nd Belorussian Front had established a bridgehead on the east bank of the Oder that was over 15 km (9 mi) deep and was heavily engaged with the III Panzer Army.[68] On 25 April, the 2nd Belorussian Front broke through III Panzer Army's line around the bridgehead south of Stettin, crossed the *Randowbruch* Swamp, and were now free to move west towards Montgomery's British 21st Army Group and north towards the Baltic port of Stralsund.[112]

The German III Panzer Army and the German XXI Army situated to the north of Berlin retreated westwards under relentless pressure from Rokossovsky's 2nd Belorussian Front, and was eventually pushed into a pocket 32 km (20 mi) wide that stretched from the Elbe to the coast.[67] To their west was the British 21st Army Group (which on 1 May broke out of its Elbe bridgehead and had raced to the coast capturing Wismar and Lübeck), to their east Rokossovsky's 2nd Belorussian Front and to the south was the United States Ninth Army which had penetrated as far east as Ludwigslust and Schwerin.[113]

South

The successes of the 1st Ukrainian Front during the first nine days of the battle meant that by 25 April, they were occupying large swathes of the area south and south-west of Berlin. Their spearheads had met elements of the 1st Belorussian Front west of Berlin, completing the investment of the city.[112] Meanwhile, the 58th Guards Rifle Division of the 5th Guards Army in 1st

Figure 7: *2nd Lt. William Robertson, US Army and Lt. Alexander Syl-
vashko, Red Army, shown in front of sign East Meets West symbolizing the
historic meeting of the Soviet and American Armies, near Torgau, Germany.*

Ukrainian Front made contact with the 69th Infantry Division (United States)
of the United States First Army near Torgau, on the Elbe River.[112] These
manoeuvres had broken the German forces south of Berlin into three parts.
The German IX Army was surrounded in the Halbe pocket.[114] Wenck's XII
Army, obeying Hitler's command of 22 April, was attempting to force its way
into Berlin from the south-west but met stiff resistance from 1st Ukrainian
Front around Potsdam.[115] Schörner's Army Group Centre was forced to withdraw from the Battle of Berlin, along its lines of communications towards
Czechoslovakia.[45]

Between 24 April and 1 May, the IX Army fought a desperate action to break
out of the pocket in an attempt to link up with the XII Army.[116] Hitler assumed
that after a successful breakout from the pocket, the IX Army could combine
forces with the XII Army and would be able to relieve Berlin.[117] There is no
evidence to suggest that Generals Heinrici, Busse, or Wenck thought that this
was even remotely strategically feasible, but Hitler's agreement to allow the IX
Army to break through Soviet lines allowed many German soldiers to escape
to the west and surrender to the United States Army.[118]

At dawn on 28 April, the youth divisions *Clausewitz*, *Scharnhorst*, and
Theodor Körner, attacked from the south-west toward the direction of Berlin.
They were part of Wenck's XX Corps and were made up of men from the

officer training schools, making them some of the best units the Germans had in reserve. They covered a distance of about 24 km (15 mi), before being halted at the tip of Lake Schwielow, south-west of Potsdam and still 32 km (20 mi) from Berlin.[119] During the night, General Wenck reported to the German Supreme Army Command in Fuerstenberg that his XII Army had been forced back along the entire front. According to Wenck, no attack on Berlin was possible.[120,121] At that point, support from the IX Army could no longer be expected.[102] In the meantime, about 25,000 German soldiers of the IX Army, along with several thousand civilians, succeeded in reaching the lines of the XII Army after breaking out of the Halbe pocket.[122] The casualties on both sides were very high. Nearly 30,000 Germans were buried after the battle in the cemetery at Halbe.[56] About 20,000 soldiers of the Red Army also died trying to stop the breakout; most are buried at a cemetery next to the Baruth-Zossen road.[56] These are the known dead, but the remains of more who died in the battle are found every year, so the total of those who died will never be known. Nobody knows how many civilians died but it could have been as high as 10,000.[56]

Having failed to break through to Berlin, Wenck's XII Army made a fighting retreat back towards the Elbe and American lines after providing the IX Army survivors with surplus transport.[123] By 6 May many German Army units and individuals had crossed the Elbe and surrendered to the US Ninth Army.[111] Meanwhile, the XII Army's bridgehead, with its headquarters in the park of Schönhausen, came under heavy Soviet artillery bombardment and was compressed into an area eight by two kilometres (five by one and a quarter miles).[124]

Surrender

On the night of 2–3 May, General Hasso von Manteuffel, commander of the III Panzer Army along with General Kurt von Tippelskirch, commander of the XXI Army, surrendered to the US Army.[111] Von Saucken's II Army, that had been fighting north-east of Berlin in the Vistula Delta, surrendered to the Soviets on 9 May.[113] On the morning of 7 May, the perimeter of the XII Army's bridgehead began to collapse. Wenck crossed the Elbe under small arms fire that afternoon and surrendered to the American Ninth Army.[124]

Aftermath

According to Grigoriy Krivosheev's work based on declassified archival data, Soviet forces sustained 81,116 dead for the entire operation, which included the battles of Seelow Heights and the Halbe;[11] Another 280,251 were reported wounded or sick during the operational period[125] The operation also cost the

Figure 8: *A devastated street in the city centre just off the Unter den Linden, 3 July 1945.*

Soviets about 1,997 tanks and SPGs.[12] Krivosheev noted: "All losses of arms and equipment are counted as irrecoverable losses, i.e. beyond economic repair or no longer serviceable".[126] Soviet estimates based on kill claims placed German losses at 458,080 killed and 479,298 captured,[127] but German research puts the number of dead at approximately 92,000 – 100,000.[13] The number of civilian casualties is unknown, but 125,000 are estimated to have perished during the entire operation.[128]

In those areas which the Red Army had captured and before the fighting in the centre of the city had stopped, the Soviet authorities took measures to start restoring essential services.[129] Almost all transport in and out of the city had been rendered inoperative, and bombed-out sewers had contaminated the city's water supplies.[130] The Soviet authorities appointed local Germans to head each city block, and organised the cleaning-up.[129] The Red Army made a major effort to feed the residents of the city.[129] Most Germans, both soldiers and civilians, were grateful to receive food issued at Red Army soup kitchens which began on Colonel-General Nikolai Berzarin's orders.[131] After the capitulation the Soviets went house to house, arresting and imprisoning anyone in a uniform including firemen and railwaymen.[132]

During, and in the days immediately following the assault,[133,134] in many areas of the city, vengeful Soviet troops (often rear echelon units[135]) engaged in mass

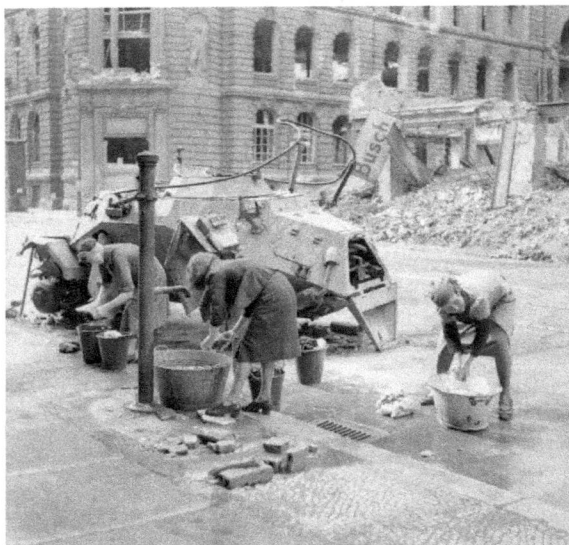

Figure 9: *German women washing clothes at a water hydrant in a Berlin street. A knocked-out German scout car stands beside them, 3 July 1945.*

rape, pillage and murder.[136] Oleg Budnitskii, historian at the Higher School of Economics in Moscow, told a BBC Radio programme that Red Army soldiers were astounded when they reached Germany. "For the first time in their lives, eight million Soviet people came abroad, the Soviet Union was a closed country. All they knew about foreign countries was there was unemployment, starvation and exploitation. And when they came to Europe they saw something very different from Stalinist Russia... especially Germany. They were really furious, they could not understand why being so rich, Germans came to Russia".[137]

Despite Soviet efforts to supply food and rebuild the city, starvation remained a problem.[130] In June 1945, one month after the surrender, the average Berliner was getting only 64 percent of a daily ration of 1,240 calories (5,200 kJ).[138] Across the city over a million people were without homes.[139]

Commemoration

1,100,000 Soviet personnel who took part in the capture of Berlin from 22 April to 2 May 1945 were awarded with the Medal "For the Capture of Berlin".[140]

Figure 10: *"Victory Banner #5", raised on the roof of the Reichstag.*

Figure 11: *Polish flag raised on the top of Berlin Victory Column on May 2, 1945.*

The Victory Banner to be used for celebrations of the Soviet Victory Day was defined by a federal law of Russia,[141] on 7 May 2007, as a copy of the flag was raised on the Reichstag (with the hammer and sickle, and the inscription)Wikipedia:Citation needed.

Poland's official Flag Day is held each year on 2 May, the last day of the battle in Berlin, when the Polish Army hoisted its flag on the Berlin Victory Column.[142]

References

- Antill, Peter (2005), *Berlin 1945*, Osprey, ISBN 978-1-84176-915-8
- Beevor, Antony (1 May 2002), "They raped every German female from eight to 80"[143], *The Guardian*, archived[144] from the original on 5 October 2008, retrieved 13 September 2008
- Beevor, Antony (2002), *Berlin: The Downfall 1945*, Viking-Penguin Books, ISBN 978-0-670-03041-5
- Beevor, Antony (2003), *Berlin: The Downfall 1945*, Penguin Books, ISBN 978-0-14-028696-0
- Bellamy, Chris (2007), *Absolute war: Soviet Russia in the Second World War*, Alfred A. Knopf, ISBN 978-0-375-41086-4
- Bergstrom, Christer (2007), *Bagration to Berlin – The Final Air Battles in the East: 1944–1945*, Ian Allan, ISBN 978-1-903223-91-8
- Budnitskii, Oleg (3 May 2015), "Interview", *The Rape of Berlin (broadcast)*, by Ash, Lucy, BBC Radio 4
- Bullock, Alan (1962), *Hitler: A Study in Tyranny*, Penguin Books, ISBN 978-0-14-013564-0
- Clodfelter, Michael (2002), *Warfare and Armed Conflicts: A Statistical Reference to Casualty and Other Figures, 1500–2000* (2nd ed.), McFarland & Company, ISBN 978-0-7864-1204-4
- Dollinger, Hans (1967) [1965], *The Decline and Fall of Nazi Germany and Imperial Japan*, New York: Bonanza Books, ISBN 978-0517013137
- Duffy, Christopher (1991), *Red Storm on the Reich*, Routledge, ISBN 978-0-415-03589-7
- Fischer, Thomas (2008), *Soldiers of the Leibstandarte*, J.J. Fedorowicz Publishing, ISBN 978-0-921991-91-5
- Gareev, Makhmut; Tretiak, Ivan; Rzheshevsky, Oleg (21 July 2005), interviewed by Sergey Turchenko, "Насилие над фактами" [Abuse of Facts], *Trud* (in Russian)
- Glantz, David M. (1998), *When Titans Clashed: How the Red Army Stopped Hitler*, University Press of Kansas, ISBN 978-0-7006-0899-7
- Glantz, David M. (11 October 2001), *The Soviet-German War 1941–1945: Myths and Realities: A Survey Essay*[145], The Strom Thurmond Institute, archived from the original[146] on 18 February 2015

• Gregory, Don A.; Gehlen, William R. (2009), *Two Soldiers, Two Lost Fronts: German War Diaries of the Stalingrad and North Africa Campaigns* (illustrated ed.), Casemate Publishers, pp. 207,208[147], ISBN 978-1-935149-05-7

• Grossmann, Atina (2009), *Jews, Germans, and Allies: Close Encounters in Occupied Germany*, Princeton University Press, ISBN 978-0-691-14317-0

• Hamilton, A. Stephan (2008), *Bloody Streets: The Soviet Assault on Berlin, April 1945*, Helion & Co., ISBN 978-1-906033-12-5

• Hastings, Max (2004), *Armageddon: The Battle for Germany, 1944–1945*, Macmillan, ISBN 978-0-333-90836-5

• Hastings, Max (2005), *Armageddon: The Battle for Germany, 1944–1945*, Pan, ISBN 978-0-330-49062-7

• Isaev, Aleksey (26 July 2010), "Seelow Heights"[148], *Price of Victory* (Interview) (in Russian), interviewed by Vitaly Dymarsky, Moscow: Echo of Moscow, retrieved December 2012 Check date values in: |access-date= (help)

• Ketchum, M. (6 December 2014), *The WW2 Letters of Private Melvin W. Johnson*[149], KetchCetera, retrieved December 2014 Check date values in: |accessdate= (help)

• Komorowski, Krzysztof (2009), "Boje polskie 1939–1945: przewodnik encyklopedyczny"[150], *Wojskowe Biuro Badań Historycznych*, Poland: Bellona, pp. 65–67, ISBN 978-83-7399-353-2, retrieved 12 May 2011

• Krivosheev, G. F. (1997), *Soviet Casualties and Combat Losses in the Twentieth Century*, Greenhill Books, ISBN 978-1-85367-280-4

• Kutylowski, Denny (21 November 2011), *Polish Holidays*[151], Polish Toledo

• Lavrenov, Sergei; Popov, Igor (2000), <bdi lang="ru" >Крах Третьего рейха</bdi> [*The Fall of the Third Reich*] (in Russian), Moscow: ACT, ISBN 5-237-05065-4

• Le Tissier, Tony (2005), *Slaughter at Halbe*, Sutton, ISBN 978-0-7509-3689-7

• Lewis, John E. (1998), *The Mammoth Book of Eye-witness History*, Pgw, ISBN 978-0-7867-0534-4

• McInnis, Edgar (1946), *The war*, **6**, Oxford University Press

• Milward, Alan S. (1980), *War, Economy and Society, 1939–1945*, University of California Press, ISBN 978-0-520-03942-1

• Müller, Rolf-Dieter (2008), *Das Deutsche Reich und der Zweite Weltkrieg, Band 10/1: Der Zusammenbruch des Deutschen Reiches 1945 und die Folgen des Zweiten Weltkrieges – Teilbd 1: Die militärische Niederwerfung der Wehrmacht* (in German), Deutsche Verlags-Anstalt, ISBN 978-3-421-06237-6

- Murray, Williamson; Millett, Allan Reed (2000), *A War to be Won*, Harvard University Press, ISBN 978-0-674-00680-5
- RAF staff (13 March 2006), *RAF History — Bomber Command 60th Anniversary*[152], RAF, archived from the original[153] on 28 July 2012, retrieved April 2012 Check date values in: | accessdate= (help)
- *Федеральный закон Российской Федерации от 7 мая 2007 г. N 68-ФЗ "О Знамени Победы" (Federal Law of the Russian Federation dated May 7, 2007 N 68 -FZ "On the Banner of Victory")*[154] (in Russian), rg.ru, 8 May 2007, archived[155] from the original on 19 May 2011, retrieved June 2011 Check date values in: | accessdate= (help)
- Ryan, Cornelius (1966), *The Last Battle*, Simon & Schuster, ISBN 978-0-671-40640-0
- Rzheshevsky, Oleg A. (2002), <bdi lang="ru" >Берлинская операция 1945 г.: дискуссия продолжается</bdi> [The Berlin Operation of 1945: Discussion Continues], *Мир истории* [*World of History*] (in Russian) (4)
- Simons, Gerald (1982), *Victory in Europe*, Time-Life Books, ISBN 978-0-8094-3406-0
- Sontheimer, Michael (7 May 2008), "Iconic Red Army Reichstag Photo Faked"[156], *Spiegel Online*, archived[157] from the original on 13 September 2008, retrieved 13 September 2008
- Tiemann, Ralf (1998), *The Leibstandarte IV/2*, J.J. Fedorowicz Publishing, ISBN 978-0-921991-40-3
- Wagner, Ray (1974), *The Soviet Air Force in World War II: the Official History*, Doubleday
- White, Osmar (2003), *Conquerors' Road: An Eyewitness Report of Germany 1945*, Cambridge University Press, ISBN 978-0-521-53751-3
- Williams, Andrew (2005), *D-Day to Berlin*, Hodder, ISBN 978-0-340-83397-1
- Zaloga, Steven J. (1982), *'The Polish Army, 1939–45*, Osprey Publishing
- Ziemke, Earl F. (1969), *Battle for Berlin End of the Third Reich Ballantine's Illustrated History of World War II (Battle Book #6)*, Ballantine Books
- Ziemke, Earl F. (1990), "Chapter 17 Zone and Sector"[158], *The U.S. Army in the occupation of Germany 1944–1946*[159], Washington, D. C.: Center of Military History, United States Army, Library of Congress Catalog Card Number 75-619027
- Ziemke, Earl F. (1983), "Germany and World War II: The Official History?", *Central European History*, **16** (4): 398–407, doi: 10.1017/S0008938900001266[160]
- Zuljan, Ralph (1 July 2003), *Battle for the Seelow Heights – Part II*[161], archived from the original[162] on 25 May 2011 Originally published in "World War II" at Suite101.com on 1 May 1999. Revised edition pub-

lished in "Articles On War" at OnWar.com[163] on 1 July 2003.

Further reading

Wikisourcehas original text related to this article:
Adolf Hitler's Order for a Last Stand in the East

- Antill, P., *Battle for Berlin: April – May 1945*[164] — Includes the Order of Battle for the Battle for Berlin (Le Tissier, T. (1988), *The Battle of Berlin 1945*, London: Jonathan Cape)
- Durie, W. (2012), *The British Garrison Berlin 1945–1994: No Where to Go*, Berlin: Vergangenheits/Berlin, ISBN 978-3-86408-068-5
- Erickson, John (1983), *The Road to Berlin: Continuing the History of Stalin's War with Germany*, Westview Press, ISBN 978-0-89158-795-8
- Anonymous; *A Woman in Berlin: Six Weeks in the Conquered City* Translated by Anthes Bell, ISBN 978-0-8050-7540-3
- Kuby, Erich (1968), *The Russians and Berlin, 1945*, Hill and Wang
- Moeller, Robert G. (1997), *West Germany Under Construction*, University of Michigan Press, ISBN 978-0-472-06648-3
- Naimark, Norman M. (1995), *The Russians in Germany: A History of the Soviet Zone of Occupation, 1945–1949*, Cambridge: Belknap, ISBN 978-0-674-78405-5
- Read, Anthony; Fisher, David (1993), *The Fall of Berlin*, London: Pimlico, ISBN 978-0-7126-0695-0
- Sanders, Ian J., *Photos of World War 2 Berlin Locations today*[165], archived from the original[166] on 14 October 2007
- Shepardson, Donald E. (1998), "The Fall of Berlin and the Rise of a Myth", *The Journal of Military History*, **62** (1): 135–153
- Tilman, Remme, *The Battle for Berlin in World War Two*[167], BBC
- White, Osmar, *By the eyes of a war correspondent*[168], archived from the original[169] on 18 March 2007 — Alternative account of crimes against civilians
- RT (TV network), (official channel on YouTube). "Fall of Berlin: Stopping the Nazi Heart"[170] on YouTube. 27 June 2010. 26-minute video.

Preparations

Order of battle for the Battle of Berlin

This is the order of battle that took place on April 16, 1945, in the end stages of World War II, between the German Wehrmacht and the Soviet Red Army. This battle took place before the start of the Battle of the Oder–Neisse and concluded with the Battle in Berlin. Units are listed as they were deployed from North to South before the start of the Battle of the Seelow Heights.

Germans

Army Group Vistula

Colonel General **Gotthard Heinrici**

Third Panzer Army

General of Panzer **Hasso von Manteuffel**

    Swinemunde Corps - General of Infantry **John Ansat**

        2nd Naval Division

        402nd Naval Division

    XXXII Corps - General of Infantry **Friedrich-August Schack**

        Voigt Infantry Divisions

        281st Infantry Divisions

        549th Volksgrenadier Division

    Oder Corps - Obergruppenführer **Erich von dem Bach-Zelewski**

        Klossek Infantry Divisions

        610th Infantry Divisions

    XXXXVI Panzer Corps - General of Infantry **Martin Gareis**

        547th Volksgrenadier Division

        1st Naval Division

Figure 12: *Berlin operation*

Ninth Army

General of Infantry **Theodor Busse**

    CI Corps - General of Artillery **Wilhelm Berlin**

        5th Jäger Division

        309th *Berlin* Infantry Division

        25th Panzergrenadier Division

        Kampfgruppe *1001 Nights*

    LVI Panzer Corps - General of Artillery **Helmuth Weidling**

        9th Fallschirmjäger Division

        18th Panzergrenadier Division *(Originally with OKW)*

        20th Panzergrenadier Division

        Müncheberg Panzer Division

    XI SS Panzer Corps - Obergruppenführer **Matthias Kleinheisterkamp**

        303rd 'Döberitz' Infantry Division

        169th Infantry Division

712th Infantry Division

Kurmark Panzergrenadier Division

V SS Mountain Corps - Obergruppenführer **Friedrich Jeckeln**

286th Infantry Division

32nd SS Grenadier Division

391st Security Division

Army Group Reserve

III SS Panzer Corps - Obergruppenführer **Felix Steiner**

(Divisions later allocated to the 9th Army)

11th SS Panzergrenadier Division

23rd SS Panzergrenadier Division

(Divisions later allocated to the 3rd Panzer Army)

27th SS Grenadier Division

28th SS Grenadier Division

Army Group Centre

Feldmarshal **Ferdinand Schörner**

Fourth Panzer Army

General of Panzer **Fritz-Hubert Gräser**

(Later transferred to the 9th Army)

V Corps - General of Artillery **Kurt Wäger**

35th SS Police Grenadier Division

36th SS Grenadier Division

275th Infantry Division

342nd Infantry Division

21st Panzer Division

Twelfth Army

General of Panzer **Walther Wenck**

   XX Corps - General of Cavalry **Carl-Erik Koehler**

      Theodor Körner RAD Infantry Division

      Ulrich von Hutten Infantry Division

      Ferdinand von Schill Infantry Division

      Scharnhorst Infantry Division

   XXXIX Panzer Corps - Lt. Gen. **Karl Arndt**

(12 – 21 April 1945 under OKW with the following structure)

      Clausewitz Panzer Division

      Schlageter RAD Division

      84th Infantry Division

(21 – 26 April 1945 under 12th Army with the following structure)

      Clausewitz Panzer Division

      84th Infantry Division

      Hamburg Reserve Infantry Division

      Meyer Infantry Division

   XXXXI Panzer Corps - Lt. Gen. **Rudolf Holste**

      Von Hake Infantry Division

      199th Infantry Division

      V-Weapons Infantry Division

   XLVIII Panzer Corps - General of Panzer **Maximilian von Edelsheim**

      14th Flak Division

      Kampfgruppe *Leipzig*

      Kampfgruppe *Halle*

Soviets

2nd Belorussian Front[171]

Marshal **Konstantin Rokossovsky**

2nd Shock Army
Colonel General **Ivan Fedyuninsky**
108th Rifle Corps
46th Rifle Division
90th Rifle Division
372nd Rifle Division
116th Rifle Corps
86th Rifle Division
321st Rifle Division
326th Rifle Division

65th Army
Colonel General **Pavel Batov**
18th Rifle Corps
15th Rifle Division
37th Guards Rifle Division
69th Rifle Division
46th Rifle Corps
108th Rifle Division
186th Rifle Division
413th Rifle Division
105th Rifle Corps
44th Guards Rifle Division
193rd Rifle Division
354th Rifle Division

70th Army
Colonel General **V. S. Popov**
47th Rifle Corps
71st Rifle Division
136th Rifle Division
162nd Rifle Division
96th Rifle Corps
1st Rifle Division
38th Guards Rifle Division
165th Rifle Division
114th Rifle Corps
76th Guards Rifle Division
160th Rifle Division
300th Rifle Division

49th Army
Colonel General **I. T. Grishin**
70th Rifle Corps
139th Rifle Division
238th Rifle Division
121st Rifle Corps
42nd Rifle Division
199th Rifle Division
380th Rifle Division

19th Army
Colonel General **Romanowsky W.Z.**
40th Guards Rifle Corps
10th Guards Rifle Division
101st Guards Rifle Division
102nd Guards Rifle Division
132nd Rifle Corps
18th Rifle Division
27th Rifle Division
313th Rifle Division
134th Rifle Corps
205th Rifle Division
272nd Rifle Division
310th Rifle Division

5th Guards Tank Army
Colonel General **Vasily Volsky**
29th Tank Corps
53rd Motorized Rifle Brigade
25th Tank Brigade
31st Tank Brigade
32nd Tank Brigade

1st Belorussian Front[172]

Marshal **Georgy Zhukov**

61st Army
Colonel General **P. A. Belov**
9th Guards Rifle Corps
12th Rifle Division
415th Rifle Division
75th Guards Rifle
Division
80th Rifle Corps
212th Rifle Division
234th Rifle Division
356th Rifle Division
89th Rifle Corps
23rd Rifle Division
311th Rifle Division
397th Rifle Division

1st Polish Army
Lieutenant General
Stanislav Poplavsky
Polish 1st In-
fantry Division
Polish 2nd In-
fantry Division
Polish 3rd In-
fantry Division
Polish 4th In-
fantry Division
Polish 6th In-
fantry Division
Polish 1st
Armoured
Brigade

47th Army
Colonel General **F. I. Perkhorovitch**
77th Rifle Corps
185th Rifle Division
260th Rifle Division
328th Rifle Division
125th Rifle Corps
60th Rifle Division
76th Rifle Division
175th Rifle Division
129th Rifle Corps
82nd Rifle Division
132nd Rifle Division
143rd Rifle Division

3rd Shock Army
Colonel General **Vasily Kuznetsov**
7th Rifle Corps
146th Rifle Division
265th Rifle Division
365th Rifle Division
12th Guards Rifle Corps
23rd Guards Rifle
Division
33rd Rifle Division
52nd Guards Rifle
Division
79th Rifle Corps
150th Rifle Division
171st Rifle Division
207th Rifle Division
9th Tank Corps
8th Motorized Rifle
Brigade
23rd Tank Brigade
95th Tank Brigade
108th Tank Brigade

5th Shock Army
Colonel General **Nikolai Berzarin**
9th Rifle Corps
230th Rifle
Division
248th Rifle
Division
301st Rifle
Division
26th Guards Rifle Corps
89th Guards Rifle
Division
94th Guards Rifle
Division
266th Rifle
Division
32nd Rifle Corps
60th Guards Rifle
Division
295th Rifle
Division
416th Rifle
Division

8th Guards Army
Colonel Generall **Vasily Chuikov**
4th Guards Rifle Corps
35th Guards Rifle
Division
47th Guards Rifle
Division
57th Guards Rifle
Division
28th Guards Rifle Corps
39th Guards Rifle
Division
79th Guards Rifle
Division
88th Guards Rifle
Division
29th Guards Rifle Corps
27th Guards Rifle
Division
74th Guards Rifle
Division
82nd Guards Rifle
Division

69th Army

Colonel General **Vladimir Kolpakchi**
- **25th Rifle Corps**
  - 4th Rifle Division
  - 77th Guards Rifle Division
- **61st Rifle Corps**
  - 134th Rifle Division
  - 246th Rifle Division
  - 247th Rifle Division
- **91st Rifle Corps**
  - 41st Rifle Division
  - 312th Rifle Division
  - 370th Rifle Division

33rd Army

Colonel General **V.D. Svotaev**
- **16th Rifle Corps**
  - 323rd Rifle Division
  - 339th Rifle Division
  - 383rd Rifle Division
- **38th Rifle Corps**
  - 52nd Rifle Division
  - 64th Rifle Division
  - 89th Rifle Division
  - 169th Rifle Division
- **62nd Rifle Corps**
  - 49th Rifle Division
  - 222nd Rifle Division
  - 362nd Rifle Division
- **2nd Guards Cavalry Corps**
  - 3rd Guards Cavalry Division
  - 4th Guards Cavalry Division
  - 17th Guards Cavalry Division

1st Guards Tank Army

Colonel General **Mikhail Katukov**
- **8th Guards Mechanized Corps**
  - 19th Guards Mechanized Brigade
  - 20th Guards Mechanized Brigade
  - 21st Guards Mechanized Brigade
  - 1st Guards Tank Brigade
- **11th Guards Tank Corps**
  - 27th Guards Mechanized Brigade
  - 40th Guards Tank Brigade
  - 44th Guards Tank Brigade
  - 45th Guards Tank Brigade
- **11th Tank Corps**
  - 12th Motorized Rifle Brigade
  - 20th Tank Brigade
  - 36th Tank Brigade
  - 65th Tank Brigade

2nd Guards Tank Army

Colonel General **Semen Bogdanov**
- **1st Mechanized Corps**
  - 19th Mechanized Brigade
  - 35th Mechanized Brigade
  - 37th Mechanized Brigade
  - 219th Tank Brigade
- **9th Guards Tank Corps**
  - 33rd Guards Mechanized Brigade
  - 47th Guards Tank Brigade
  - 50th Guards Tank Brigade
  - 65th Guards Tank Brigade
- **12th Guards Tank Corps**
  - 34th Guards Mechanized Brigade
  - 48th Guards Tank Brigade
  - 49th Guards Tank Brigade
  - 66th Guards Tank Brigade

3rd Army

Colonel General **Alexander Gorbatov**
- **35th Rifle Corps**
  - 250th Rifle Division
  - 290th Rifle Division
  - 348th Rifle Division
- **40th Rifle Corps**
  - 5th Rifle Division
  - 129th Rifle Division
- **41st Rifle Corps**
  - 120th Rifle Division
  - 269th Rifle Division

1st Ukrainian Front[173]

Marshal **Ivan Konev**

3rd Guards Army
Colonel General **V. N. Gordov**
21st Rifle Corps
58th Rifle Division
253rd Rifle
Division
329th Rifle
Division
76th Rifle Corps
106th Rifle
Division
187th Rifle
Division
120th Rifle Corps
127th Rifle
Division
149th Rifle
Division
197th Rifle
Division
25th Tank Corps
20th Motorized
Rifle Brigade
111th Tank Brigade
162nd Tank
Brigade
175th Tank Brigade

13th Army
Colonel General **N. P. Phukov**
24th Rifle Corps
121st Guards
Rifle Division
395th Rifle
Division
27th Rifle Corps
6th Guards Rifle
Division
280th Rifle
Division
350th Rifle
Division
102nd Rifle Corps
117th Guards
Rifle Division
147th Rifle
Division
172nd Rifle
Division

5th Guards Army
Colonel General **Aleksei Semenovich Zhadov**
32nd Guards Rifle Corps
13th Guards Rifle
Division
95th Guards Rifle
Division
97th Guards Rifle
Division
33rd Guards Rifle Corps
9th Guards Airborne
Division
78th Guards Rifle
Division
118th Rifle Division
34th Guards Rifle Corps
14th Guards Rifle
Division
15th Guards Rifle
Division
58th Guards Rifle
Division
4th Guards Tank Corps
3rd Guards Motorized
Rifle Brigade
12th Guards Tank
Brigade
13th Guards Tank
Brigade
14th Guards Tank
Brigade

2nd Polish Army
Lt General **Karol Świerczewski**
Polish 5th
Infantry
Division
Polish 7th
Infantry
Division
Polish 8th
Infantry
Division
Polish 9th
Infantry
Division
Polish 10th
Infantry
Division
Polish 1st Armored Corps

52nd Army
Colonel General **K. A. Koroteyev**
48th Rifle Corps
116th Rifle Division
294th Rifle Division
73rd Rifle Corps
50th Rifle Division
111th Rifle Division
254th Rifle Division
78th Rifle Corps
31st Rifle Division
214th Rifle Division
373rd Rifle Division
7th Guards Mechanised Corps
24th Guards Mechanized
Brigade
25th Guards Mechanized
Brigade
26th Guards Mechanized
Brigade
57th Guards Tank Brigade

3rd Guards Tank Army
Colonel General **Pavel Rybalko**
9th Mechanized Corps
69th Mechanized Brigade
70th Mechanized Brigade
71st Mechanized Brigade
91st Tank Brigade
6th Guards Tank Corps
22nd Guards Motorized
Rifle Brigade
51st Guards Tank Brigade
52nd Guards Tank Brigade
53rd Guards Tank Brigade
7th Guards Tank Corps
23rd Guards Motorized
Rifle Brigade
54th Guards Tank Brigade
55th Guards Tank Brigade
56th Guards Tank Brigade

4th Guards Tanks Army

Colonel General **Dmitry Lelyushenko**

5th Guards Mechanized Corps
10th Guards Mechanized Brigade
11th Guards Mechanized Brigade
12th Guards Mechanized Brigade
24th Guards Tank Brigade

6th Guards Mechanized Corps
16th Guards Mechanized Brigade
17th Guards Mechanized Brigade
35th Guards Mechanized Brigade

10th Guards Tank Corps
29th Guards Motorized Rifle Brigade
61st Guards Tank Brigade
62nd Guards Tank Brigade
63rd Guards Tank Brigade

28th Army

Colonel General **A. A. Luchinsky**

20th Rifle Corps
20th Rifle Division
48th Guards Rifle Division
55th Guards Rifle Division

38th Guards Rifle Corps
50th Guards Rifle Division
54th Guards Rifle Division
96th Guards Rifle Division

128th Rifle Corps
61st Rifle Division
130th Rifle Division
152nd Rifle Division

31st Army

Colonel General **V. K. Baranov**

1st Guards Cavalry Corps
1st Guards Cavalry Division
2nd Guards Cavalry Division
7th Guards Cavalry Division

Battle of the Oder–Neisse

Battle of the Oder–Neisse

Battle of the Oder–Neisse	
Part of the Eastern Front of the Second World War	
A modern view of the Oder-Neisse line at Usedom	
Date	April 1945
Location	Oder–Neisse, Germany 52°31′47.3"N 14°25′33.9"E[174]Coordinates: 52°31′47.3"N 14°25′33.9"E[174]
Result	Soviet/Polish victory
Belligerents	
Soviet Union Poland	Germany
Commanders and leaders	
Georgy Zhukov Vasily Chuikov	Gotthard Heinrici Ferdinand Schörner
Strength	
2,500,000	300,000
Casualties and losses	
24,000 killedWikipedia:Citation needed	50,000 killedWikipedia:Citation needed

The **Battle of the Oder–Neisse** is the German name for the initial (operational) phase of one of the last two strategic offensives conducted by the Red Army

in the Campaign in Central Europe (1 January – 9 May 1945) during World
War II. Its initial breakthrough phase was fought over four days, from 16 April
until 19 April 1945, within the larger context of the Battle of Berlin. The
Soviet military planners divide the frontal and pincer phases of the operation,
named Berlin Strategic Offensive Operation into:

   Stettin-Rostock Offensive Operation (16 April 1945 – 8 May 1945) by the
   2nd Belorussian Front

   Seelow-Berlin Offensive Operation (16 April 1945 – 2 May 1945) by the
   1st Belorussian Front

   Cottbus-Potsdam Offensive Operation (16 April 1945 – 2 May 1945) by
   the northern flank and Cavalry Mechanized Group of the 1st Ukrainian
   Front

   Spremberg-Torgau Offensive Operation (16 April 1945 – 5 May 1945) by
   the southern flank of the 1st Ukrainian Front

The battle included heavy fighting by the three Fronts of the Marshals of Soviet
Union Konstantin Rokossovsky's 2nd Belorussian Front, Georgy Zhukov's 1st
Belorussian Front and Ivan Konev's 1st Ukrainian Front, that assaulted the
defending Wehrmacht Army Group Vistula commanded by Colonel-General
(Generaloberst) Gotthard Heinrici and Field Marshal Ferdinand Schörner's
Army Group Centre.

Combat operations

Most of the fighting took place during 1st Belorussian Front's assault on the
Seelow Heights, that were defended by the German 9th Army (part of Army
Group Vistula), in what became known as the *Battle of the Seelow Heights*.
1st Ukrainian Front encountered much lighter resistance crossing the Neisse to
penetrate defensive lines of Army Group Centre.

In the early hours on 16 April 1945, the Berlin Strategic Offensive Operation began with a massive bombardment by thousands of artillery pieces and
Katyusha rockets in a barrage which was sustained for as long as two hours
on some sectors of the front.[175] Shortly afterwards and well before dawn, the
1st Belorussian Front attacked across the Oder, and the 1st Ukrainian Front
attacked across the Neisse. The 1st Belorussian Front was strengthened because it had the more difficult assignment and was facing the majority of the
German forces in prepared defences.[176,177]

Figure 13: *Soviet artillery bombarding German positions during the Battle of the Seelow Heights*

Battle of the Seelow Heights

The initial attack by the 1st Belorussian Front was a disaster; Heinrici anticipated the move and withdrew his defenders from the first line of trenches just before the Red Army artillery obliterated them. The light from 143 searchlights, which were intended to blind the defenders, was diffused by the early morning mist and made useful silhouettes of the attacking Red Army formations. The swampy ground proved to be a great hindrance and under a German counter-barrage, Red Army casualties were very heavy. Frustrated by the slow advance, or perhaps on the direct orders of the Stavka ("Headquarters"), Zhukov threw in his reserves, which in his plan were to have been held back to exploit the expected breakthrough. By early evening, an advance of almost six kilometres had been achieved in some areas, but the German lines remained relatively intact.

Zhukov was forced to report that the Seelow Heights offensive was not going as planned. Stalin, to spur Zhukov, told him that he would give Konev permission to wheel his tank armies towards Berlin from the south.[178,179] The Red Army tactic of using a dense concentration of firepower was providing the usual results. By nightfall of 17 April, the German front before Zhukov remained unbroken, but only just.

On 18 April, both Soviet Fronts made steady progress. By nightfall, the 1st Belorussian Front had reached the third and final German line of defence.[180]

On the fourth day of the battle, 19 April, the 1st Belorussian Front broke through the final line of the Seelow Heights with nothing except severely depleted, withdrawing German formations between its troops and Berlin. The remnants of General Theodor Busse's 9th Army, which had been holding the heights, and the remaining northern flank of the 4th Panzer Army, were in danger of being enveloped by elements of the 1st Ukrainian Front.

While the 1st Belorussian Front encircled Berlin, the 1st Ukrainian Front started the battle for the city itself. Rokossovsky's 2nd Belorussian Front started his offensive to the north of Berlin. On 20 April, between Stettin and Schwedt, Rokossovsky's 2nd Belorussian Front attacked the northern flank of Army Group Vistula, held by the III Panzer Army. By 22 April, the 2nd Belorussian Front had established a bridgehead on the west bank of the Oder over 15 km deep, and was heavily engaged with the III Panzer Army.[181]

Cottbus-Potsdam Offensive Operation

In the south, the attack by the 1st Ukrainian Front was keeping to plan because Army Group Centre (under the command of General Ferdinand Schörner) was not providing as much opposition as that faced by Zhukov's troops. 4th Panzer Army on the north flank of his formation was falling back under the weight of the 1st Ukrainian Front Attack. Two Panzer divisions on the southern flank were retained in reserve for possible need in the centre of the Army Group front, and were not available for use to shore up the 4th Panzer Army. This was the turning point in the battle, because by nightfall the positions of both the Army Group Vistula and southern sectors of Army Group Centre were becoming untenable. Unless they fell back in line with the 4th Panzer Army, they faced envelopment. In effect, Konev's successful attacks on Schörner's poor defences to the south of the Seelow Heights positions were unhinging Heinrici's defence.[182,179]

On 18 April, the 1st Ukrainian Front, having captured the city of Forst, was preparing to break out into the relatively flat terrain.

Elements of the 3rd Guards, 3rd and 4th Guards Tank Armies, which were the Front's Cavalry Mechanized Group, having exploited the breach in the 4th Panzer Army sector of the front, turned north between Seyda and Jüterbog towards a meeting with the 1st Belorussian Front west of Berlin.

Spremberg-Torgau Offensive

Other Armies of the 1st Ukrainian Front's southern flank attacked west linking up with the Americans. That would be remembered later as the "meeting at Torgau" when the 58th Guards Division of the 5th Guards Army, part of 1st Ukrainian Front, made contact with the US 69th Infantry Division of the First Army near Torgau, Germany on the Elbe River.,[183] reaching the Mulde by 8 May.

Stettin-Rostock Offensive Operation

On 25 April, the second Belorussian Front broke through 3rd Panzer's line around the bridgehead south of Stettin and crossed the Randow swamp on the Gramzow area. They were now free to move west towards the British 21st Army Group, and north towards the Baltic ports of Stralsund and Rostock.

Results

By the end of 19 April, the German eastern front line north of Frankfurt around the Seelow and to the south around Frost had ceased to exist. These break-throughs allowed the two Red Army Fronts to envelop large parts of the German 9th and 4th Panzer Armies in a large pocket 37 km east of Frankfurt that attempted to follow the Oder-Spree Canal to Berlin. Attempts by the 9th Army to break out to the west would result in the Battle of Halbe.[184]

Operational statistics

The cost to the Red Army in making this initial breakthrough was very high. Between 1 April and 19 April, the Red Army lost over 2,807 tanks. During the same period, the Allies in the west lost 1,079 tanks.[185]

References

- Beevor, Antony. *Berlin: the Downfall, 1945*, ISBN 0-670-88695-5
- Ziemke, Earl F. *Battle For Berlin: End of the Third Reich*, NY:Ballantine Books, London:Macdomald & Co, 1969.

Battle in Berlin

Battle in Berlin

Battle in Berlin	
Part of the Battle of Berlin	
The Reichstag after the battle	
Date	23 April – 2 May 1945
Location	Berlin, Germany
	52°31′7″N 13°22′34″E[186]Coordinates: 52°31′7″N 13°22′34″E[186]
Result	Soviet victory
Belligerents	
Germany	Soviet Union
	Poland
Commanders and leaders	
Berlin Defence Area:	Georgiy Zhukov (1st Belorussian Front)
• Helmuth Reymann	Ivan Konev (1st Ukrainian Front)
• Helmuth Weidling	
Strength	
Inside the Berlin Defence Area approximately 45,000 soldiers, supplemented by the police force, Hitler Youth, and 40,000 *Volkssturm*.[187]	For the investment and assault on the Berlin Defence Area about 1,500,000 soldiers.[188]

Casualties and losses	
• 100,000 military dead • 175,000 civilians dead.[189]	75,000 dead, 300,000 wounded.[190]

The battle in Berlin was an end phase of the Battle of Berlin. While the Battle *of* Berlin encompassed the attack by three Soviet Army Groups to capture not only Berlin but the territory of Germany east of the River Elbe still under German control, the battle *in* Berlin details the fighting and German capitulation that took place within the city.

The outcome of the battle to capture the capital of the Third Reich was decided during the initial phases of the Battle of Berlin that took place outside the city. As the Soviets invested Berlin and the German forces placed to stop them were destroyed or forced back, the city's fate was sealed. Nevertheless, there was much heavy fighting within the city as the Red Army fought its way, street by street, into the centre.

On 23 April 1945, the first Soviet ground forces started to penetrate the outer suburbs of Berlin. By 27 April, Berlin was completely cut off from the outside world. The battle in the city continued until 2 May 1945. On that date, the commander of the Berlin Defence Area, General Helmuth Weidling, surrendered to the commander of the Soviet 8th Guards Army, Lieutenant-General Vasily Chuikov. Chuikov was a constituent of Marshal Georgiy Zhukov's 1st Belorussian Front.

Prelude

Battle of the Oder–Neisse

The sector in which most of the fighting in the overall battle took place was the Seelow Heights, the last major defensive line outside Berlin. The Battle of the Seelow Heights was one of the last pitched battles of World War II. It was fought over four days, from 16 April until 19 April 1945. Close to one million Soviet soldiers and more than 20,000 tanks and artillery pieces were in action to break through the "Gates to Berlin" which was defended by about 100,000 German soldiers and 1,200 tanks and guns.[191]

On 19 April, the fourth day, the 1st Belorussian Front broke through the final line of the Seelow Heights and nothing but broken German formations lay between them and Berlin. Marshal Ivan Konev's 1st Ukrainian Front, having captured Forst the day before, was fanning out into open country. One powerful thrust was heading north-west towards Berlin while other armies headed west towards a section of United States Army front line south-west of the city who were on the Elbe.

By the end of 19 April the German eastern front line north of Frankfurt around Seelow and to the south around Forst had ceased to exist. These breakthroughs allowed the two Soviet fronts to envelop the German IX Army in a large pocket east of Frankfurt. Attempts by the IX Army to break out to the west would result in the Battle of Halbe.[191,192] The cost to the Soviet forces had been very high between 1 and 19 April, with over 2,807 tanks lost,[193] including at least 727 at the Seelow Heights.[192]

Encirclement of Berlin

On 20 April, Adolf Hitler's birthday, Soviet artillery of the 79 Rifle Corps of the 1st Belorussian Front first shelled Berlin. Thereafter, Soviet artillery continued the bombardment of Berlin and did not stop until the city surrendered. After the war, the Soviets pointed out that the weight of explosives delivered by their artillery during the battle was greater than the tonnage dropped by the Western Allied bombers on the city.[194,195] The 1st Belorussian Front advanced towards the east and north-east of the city.

The 1st Ukrainian Front had pushed through the last formations of the northern wing of General Ferdinand Schörner's Army Group Centre and had passed north of Juterbog, well over halfway to the American front line on the river Elbe at Magdeburg. To the north between Stettin and Schwedt, Konstantin Rokossovsky's 2nd Belorussian Front attacked the northern flank of General Gotthard Heinrici's Army Group Vistula, held by Hasso von Manteuffel's III Panzer Army.[192]

By 24 April, elements of the 1st Belorussian Front and the 1st Ukrainian Front had completed the encirclement of the city.[196]

The next day, 25 April, the 2nd Belorussian Front broke through III Panzer Army's line around the bridgehead south of Stettin and crossed the Rando Swamp. They were now free to move west towards the British 21st Army Group and north towards the Baltic port of Stralsund. The Soviet 58th Guards Division of Zhadov's 5th Guards Army made contact with the US 69th Infantry Division of the First Army near Torgau, Germany, on the Elbe River.[197] The Soviet investment of Berlin was consolidated with leading units probing and penetrating the *S-Bahn* defensive ring. By the end of 25 April, there was no prospect that the German defence of the city could do anything but temporarily delay the capture of the capital by the Soviets as the decisive stages of the battle had already been fought and lost by the Germans fighting outside the city.[198]

Preparation

On 20 April, Hitler ordered and the *Wehrmacht* initiated "Clausewitz", which called for the complete evacuation of all *Wehrmacht* and SS offices in Berlin; this essentially formalized Berlin's status as a frontline city.[199]

The forces available to Artillery General Helmuth Weidling for the city's defence included several severely depleted *Wehrmacht* and *Waffen-SS* divisions, in all about 45,000 men. These formations were supplemented by the police force, boys in the compulsory Hitler Youth, and the *Volkssturm*. Many of the 40,000 elderly men of the *Volkssturm* had been in the army as young men and some were veterans of World War I. Hitler appointed *SS-Brigadeführer* Wilhelm Mohnke commander of the city's central government district. Mohnke's command post was in bunkers under the Reich Chancellery. The core group of his fighting men were the 800 members of the *Leibstandarte* (1st SS-Pz.Div. LSSAH) Guard Battalion (assigned to guard the *Führer*).[200] He had a total of over 2,000 men under his command.[188,201]

Weidling organised the defences into eight sectors designated 'A' to 'H', each commanded by a colonel or a general, but most had no combat experience.[188] The XX Infantry Division was to the west of the city; the IX Parachute Division to the north; the Panzer Division *Müncheberg* (Werner Mummert) to the north-east; the XI SS *Panzergrenadier* Division *Nordland* (Joachim Ziegler) to the south-east; and to the east of Tempelhof Airport. The reserve, 18th *Panzergrenadier* Division, was in Berlin's central district.

Tactics and terrain

A Soviet combat group was a mixed arms unit of about eighty men in assault groups of six to eight soldiers, closely supported by field artillery. These were tactical units which were able to apply the tactics of house to house fighting that they had been forced to develop and refine at each *Festungsstadt* (fortress city) they had encountered since Stalingrad.[202]

The German tactics used for urban warfare in Berlin were dictated by three considerations: the experience that they had gained during five years of war, the physical characteristics of the city, and the methods used by the Soviets. Most of the central districts of Berlin consist of city blocks with straight wide roads and contain several waterways, parks and large railway marshalling yards. It is a predominantly flat area, with some low hills such as the Kreuzberg, which is 66 metres (217 ft) above sea level.[203,204,205,206] Much of the housing stock consisted of apartments blocks built in the second half of the 19th century. Most of those, thanks to housing regulations and few elevators, were five stories high and built around a courtyard that could be reached from

Figure 14: *Berlin apartment blocks in 1900.*

the street through a corridor large enough to accommodate a horse and cart or a small delivery truck. In many places, these apartment blocks were built around several courtyards, one behind the other, each reached through the outer court-yards by a ground level corridor similar to that between the first courtyard and the road. The larger, more expensive flats faced the street while the smaller, more modest dwellings were grouped around the inner courtyards.[207]

Just as the Soviets had learned a lot about urban warfare, so had the Germans. The *Waffen-SS* did not use makeshift barricades erected close to street corners, because these could be raked by artillery fire from guns firing over open sights further along the straight streets. Instead, they put snipers and machine guns on the upper floors and roofs because the Soviet tanks could not elevate their guns that high, and simultaneously they put men armed with *panzerfausts* in cellar windows to ambush tanks as they moved down the streets. These tactics were quickly adopted by the Hitler Youth and the First World War *Volkssturm* veterans.[208]

Initially Soviet tanks advanced down the middle of the streets, but to counter the German tactics, they altered their own and started to hug the sides of the streets (this allowed for supporting cross-fire from tanks either side of the wider thoroughfares).[209] The Soviets also mounted sub-machine gunners on the tanks who sprayed every doorway and window, but this meant the tank could

Figure 15: *A devastated street in the city centre, 3 July 1945*

not traverse its turret quickly. Another solution was to rely on heavy how-itzers (152 mm and 203 mm) firing over open sights to blast defended build-ings and to use anti-aircraft guns against the German gunners on the higher floors. Soviet combat groups started to move from house to house instead of directly down the streets. They moved through the apartments and cellars, blasting holes through the walls of adjacent buildings (making effective use of abandoned German *panzerfausts*), while others fought across the rooftops and through the attics. These enfilading tactics took the Germans lying in ambush for tanks in the flanks. Flamethrowers and grenades proved to be very effec-tive, but as the Berlin civilian population had not been evacuated, these tactics inevitably killed many.[208]

Battle

Outer suburbs

With the decisive stages of the battle being fought outside the city, Berlin's fate was sealed, yet the resistance inside continued.[198] On 23 April, Hitler appointed German Artillery General (*General der Artillerie*) Helmuth Wei-dling commander of the Berlin Defence Area.[210] Only a day earlier, Hitler had ordered that Weidling be executed by firing squad. This was due to a mis-understanding concerning a retreat order issued by Weidling as commander of the LVI Panzer Corps. On 20 April, Weidling had been appointed commander of the LVI Panzer Corps. Weidling replaced Lieutenant-Colonel (*Oberstleutnant*) Ernst Kaether as commander of Berlin. Only one day earlier, Kaether had replaced Lieutenant-General (*Generalleutnant*) Helmuth Reymann, who had held the position for only about a month.

By 23 April, some of Chuikov's rifle units had crossed the Spree and Dahme rivers south of Köpenick and by 24 April were advancing towards Britz and Neukölln. Accompanying them were the leading tanks of Colonel-General Mikhail Katukov's 1st Guards Tank Army. Sometime after midnight, a corps of Colonel-General Nikolai Berzarin's 5th Shock Army crossed the Spree close to Treptow Park. At dawn on 24 April the LVI Panzer Corps still under Weidling's direct command, counterattacked, but were severely mauled by the 5th Shock Army, which was able to continue its advance around mid-day.[211] Meanwhile, the first large Soviet probe into the city was put into operation. Katukov's 1st Guards Tank Army attacked across the Teltow Canal. At 06:20 a bombardment by 3,000 guns and heavy mortars began (a staggering 650 pieces of artillery per kilometer of front). At 07:00 hours the first Soviet battalions were across, to be followed by tanks around 12:00, shortly after the first of the pontoon bridges were completed. By the evening Treptow Park was in Soviet hands and they had also reached the *S-Bahn*.[212]

While the fighting raged in the south-east of the city, between 320 and 330 French volunteers commanded by *SS-Brigadeführer* Gustav Krukenberg and organised as *Sturmbataillon* (assault battalion) "Charlemagne" were attached to XI SS *Panzergrenadier* Division *Nordland*. They moved from the SS training ground near Neustrelitz to the centre of Berlin through the western suburbs, which apart from unmanned barricades across the Havel and Spree were devoid of fortifications or defenders. Of all the reinforcements ordered to Berlin that day, only this *Sturmbataillon* arrived.[198,213]

On 25 April, Krukenberg was appointed commander of Defence Sector C which included the *Nordland* Division, whose previous commander, Joachim Ziegler, was relieved of his command the same day. The arrival of the French SS men bolstered the *Nordland* Division whose *Norge* and *Danmark* regiments had been decimated in the fighting. Just midday as Krukenberg reached his command, the last German bridgehead south of the Teltow Canal was being abandoned. During the night Krukenberg informed General Hans Krebs, Chief of the General Staff of *Oberkommando des Heeres* (OKH) that within 24 hours the *Nordland* would have to fall back to the central sector Z (Z for *Zentrum* or *Mitte*).[214,215]

Figure 16: *The location of Neukölln*

Soviet combat groups of the 8th Guards Army and the 1st Guards Tank Army fought their way through the southern suburbs of Neukölln towards Tempelhof Airport which was located just inside the *S-Bahn* defensive ring. Defending Sector D was Panzer Division *Müncheberg*. This division, down to its last dozen tanks and thirty armoured personnel carriers (APC)s, had been promised replacements for battle losses but only stragglers and *Volkssturm* were available to fill the ranks. The Soviets advanced cautiously, using flamethrowers to overcome defensive positions. By dusk Soviet T-34 tanks had reached the airfield, only six kilometres (four miles) south of the *Führerbunker*, where they were checked by stiff German resistance. The *Müncheberg* Division managed to hold the line until the afternoon of the next day, but this was the last time they were able to check the Soviet advance for more than a few hours.[216,217]

On 26 April, with Neukölln heavily penetrated by Soviet combat groups, Krukenberg prepared fallback positions for Sector C defenders around Hermannplatz. He moved his headquarters into the opera house. The two understrength German divisions defending the south-east were now facing five Soviet armies. From east to west they were: the 5th Shock Army, advancing from Treptow Park; the 8th Guards Army and the 1st Guards Tank Army moving through Neukölln north (temporarily checked at Tempelhof Airport), and Colonel-General Pavel Rybalko's 3rd Guards Tank Army (part of Konev's

1st Ukrainian Front) advancing from Mariendorf. As the *Nordland* Division fell back towards Hermannplatz, the French SS and one-hundred Hitler Youth attached to their group destroyed 14 Soviet tanks with *panzerfausts*; one machine gun position by the Halensee bridge managed to hold up any Soviet advances in that area for 48 hours. The *Nordlands'* remaining armour, eight Tiger tanks and several assault guns, were ordered to take up positions in the Tiergarten, because although these two divisions of Weidling's LVI Panzer Corps could slow the Soviet advance, they could not stop it.[218] SS-*Oberscharführer* Schmidt recalled, "I was assigned as platoon leader of a 'dwindled company' which included a squad of Hungarian volunteers, *Volkssturm* men, *Hitlerjugend*, as well as members of the *Heer* [army]... Daily, the Russians advanced closer to the government quarter, which we were to defend. It became more and more difficult to hold the line 'under all circumstances'..."[219]

Hitler summoned Field Marshal Robert Ritter von Greim from Munich to Berlin to take over command of the German Air Force (*Luftwaffe*) from Hermann Göring. While flying over Berlin in a Fieseler Storch, von Greim was seriously wounded by Soviet anti-aircraft fire. Hanna Reitsch, his mistress and a crack test pilot, landed von Greim on an improvised air strip in the Tiergarten near the Brandenburg Gate.[220,221,222]

At Tempelhof Airport, the flak batteries conducted direct fire against advancing Soviet tanks until they were overrun.[223] On the following day, 27 April, 2,000 German women were rounded up and ordered to help clear Tempelhof Airport of debris so that the Red Army Air Force could start to use it.[224] Marshal Zhukov appointed Colonel-General Berzarin to start organising the German civil administration in the areas that they had captured. *Bürgermeisters*, like the directors of the Berlin utilities, were summoned to appear before Berzarin's staff.

Inner suburbs

As the Soviet armies of the 1st Belorussian Front and the 1st Ukrainian Front converged on the centre of the city there were many accidental 'friendly fire' incidents involving artillery shellings because the spotter planes and the artillery of the different Soviet Fronts were not coordinated and frequently mistook assault groups in other armies as enemy troops. Indeed, the rivalry between the Soviet armies to capture the city centre was becoming intense. A corps commander of the 1st Ukrainian Front joked with laconic humour, "Now we should be scared not of the enemy, but of our neighbour... There's nothing more depressing in Berlin than learning about the successes of your neighbour". Beevor has suggested that the rivalry went further than just jokes and says that Chuikov deliberately ordered the left flank of the 8th Guards Army (of 1st Belorussian Front) across the front of the 3rd Guards Tank Army (of

Figure 17: *Humboldthain Flak Tower in 2004*

the 1st Ukrainian Front), blocking its direct path to the Reichstag. As Chuikov did not inform Rybalko, commander of the 3rd Guards Tank Army, that the 8th was doing this, the troops ordered to carry out this manoeuvre suffered disproportionate casualties from friendly fire.[225]

In the south-west, Rybalko's 3rd Guards Tank Army, supported by Lieutenant-General Luchinsky's 28th Army, were advancing through the wooded park and suburbs of the Grunewald, attacking what remained of the XVIII *Panzergrenadier* Division on their eastern flank and entering Charlottenburg. In the south, Chuikov's 8th Guards Army and Katukov's 1st Guards Tank Army crossed the Landwehr Canal on 27 April, the last major obstacle between them and the *Führerbunker* next to the Reich Chancellery less than two kilometres away (a little over a mile). In the south-east, Berzarin's 5th Shock Army had bypassed the Friedrichshain *flak* tower and was now between Frankfurter Allee and the south bank of the Spree, where its IX Corps was fighting.[226]

By 27 April the Soviet Armies had penetrated the German's *S-Bahn* outer defensive ring from all directions. The Germans had been forced back into a pocket about twenty-five kilometres (fifteen miles) long from west to east and about three kiliometres (one and a half miles) wide at its narrowest, just west of the old city centre, near the Tiergarten. In the north-west, Lieutenant-General F.I. Perkohorovitch's 47th Army was now approaching Spandau, and was also heavily involved in a battle to capture Gatow airfield, which was defended by *Volkssturm* and Luftwaffe cadets using the feared 88 mm anti-aircraft guns in their anti-tank role. In the north, Colonel-General Semyon Bogdanov's 2nd Guards Tank Army was bogged down just south of Siemensstadt. Colonel-General Vasily Kuznetsov's 3rd Shock Army had bypassed the Humboldthain flak tower (leaving it to follow-up forces), and had reached the north of the Tiergarten and Prenzlauerberg.[227,226]

On the morning of 27 April, the Soviets continued the assault with a heavy bombardment of the inner city. The 8th Guards Army and the 1st Guards Tank Army were ordered to take Belle-Alliance-Platz (Belle-Alliance being an alternative name for the Battle of Waterloo) that in a twist of history was defended by French SS soldiers of *Sturmbataillon* "Charlemagne" attached to the *Nordland* Division. That night Weidling gave a battle situation report to Hitler, and presented him with a detailed breakout plan which would be spearheaded with just under forty tanks (all the combat-ready German tanks available in Berlin). Hitler rejected the plan, saying he would stay in the bunker and that Weidling would carry on with the defence.[228]

In sector Z (centre) Krukenberg *Nordland* divisional headquarters was now a carriage in the *Stadtmitte U-Bahn* station. The *Nordland's* armour was reduced to four captured Soviet APCs and two half-tracks, so Kruneberg's men's chief weapon was now the *panzerfaust* which were used for close quarters battle against both Soviet armour and in house to house fighting against Soviet combat groups.[229]

At dawn on 28 April, the youth divisions *Clausewitz*, *Scharnhorst* and *Theodor Körner*, attacked from the south-west in the direction of Berlin. They were part of Wenck's XX Corps and were made up of men from the officer training schools, making them some of the best units the Germans had left. They covered a distance of about 24 km (15 mi), before being halted at the tip of Lake Schwielow south-west of Potsdam and still 32 km (20 mi) from Berlin.[230] In the evening of 28 April, the BBC broadcast a Reuters news report about Heinrich Himmler's attempted negotiations with the western Allies through Count Folke Bernadotte in Luebeck. Upon being informed, Hitler flew into a rage and told those who were still with him in the bunker complex that Himmler's act was the worst treachery he had ever known.[231] Hitler ordered von Greim and Reitsch to fly to Karl Dönitz's headquarters at Ploen and arrest the "traitor" Himmler.[220]

By 28 April, the *Müncheberg* Division had been driven back to the Anhalter railway station less than 1 km (1,100 yd) south of the *Führerbunker*. To slow the advancing Soviets, allegedly on Hitler's orders, the bulkheads under the Landwehr Canal were blown up. It caused panic in the *U-Bahn* tunnels under the Anhalter railway station in which some were trampled to death. But the water level only suddenly rose by about a metre (yard) and after that much more slowly. Initially it was thought that many thousands had drowned, but when the tunnels were pumped out in October 1945 it was found that most of the bodies were of people who had died of their wounds, not from drowning.[232,233] In any event, the Soviets continued their advance with three T-34s, making it as far as Wilhelmstrasse *U-Bahn* station before being ambushed and destroyed by the Frenchmen of the *Nordland* Division.[234]

During 27 and 28 April, most of the formations of Konev's 1st Ukrainian Front that were engaged in the Battle in Berlin were ordered to disengage and proceed south to take part in the Prague Offensive (the last great offensive of the European theatre). This did not mitigate their resentment at being denied the honour of capturing the centre of Berlin, but left the 1st Belorussian Front under Marshal Zhukov to claim that honour for themselves alone.[235]

By 28 April, the Germans were now reduced to a strip less than 5 km (3.1 mi) wide and 15 km (9.3 mi) in length, from Alexanderplatz in the east to Charlottenburg and the area around the Olympic Stadium (*Reichssportfeld*) in the west. Generally, the Soviets avoided fighting their way into tunnels and bunkers (of which there were about 1,000 in the Berlin area); instead, they sealed them off and continued the advance. However, just over 1 km (0.62 mi) to the north of the *Reichstag* the 3rd Shock Army did use heavy guns at point blank range to blast a hole in the walls of Moabit prison; after a breach was made and the prison stormed, the garrison there quickly surrendered. The 3rd Shock Army were in sight of the Victory Column in the Tiergarten and during the afternoon advanced towards the Moltke bridge over the Spree, just north of the Ministry of the Interior and a mere 600 m (660 yd) from the *Reichstag*.[236] German demolition charges damaged the Moltke bridge but left it still passable to infantry. As dusk fell and under heavy artillery bombardment, the first Soviet troops crossed the bridge. By midnight, the Soviet 150th and 171st rifle divisions had secured the bridgehead against any counterattack the Germans could muster.[237]

Centre

On 28 April, Krebs made his last telephone call from the *Führerbunker*. He called Field Marshal Wilhelm Keitel, the Chief of OKW (German Armed Forces High Command), in Fürstenberg. Krebs told Keitel that, if relief did not arrive within 48 hours, all would be lost. Keitel promised to exert the utmost pressure on Generals Walther Wenck, commander of XII Army, and Theodor Busse, commander of the IX Army. Meanwhile, Martin Bormann wired to German Admiral Dönitz: [the] "Reich Chancellery (*Reichskanzlei*) [is] a heap of rubble."[220] He went on to say that the foreign press was reporting fresh acts of treason and "that without exception Schörner, Wenck and the others must

Figure 18: *The Moltke bridge around 1900*

give evidence of their loyalty by the quickest relief of the Führer".[230] Bormann was the head of the Nazi Party Chancellery (*Parteikanzlei*) and Hitler's private secretary.

During the evening, von Greim and Reitsch flew out from Berlin in an Arado Ar 96 trainer. Von Greim was ordered to get the Luftwaffe to attack the Soviet forces that had just reached Potsdamerplatz and to make sure that Himmler was punished.[238] Fearing that Hitler was escaping in the plane, troops of the Soviet 3rd Shock Army, which was fighting its way through the Tiergarten from the north, tried to shoot the Arado down. The Soviet troops failed in their efforts and the plane took off successfully.[232,239]

During the night of 28 April, Wenck reported to Keitel that his XII Army had been forced back along the entire front. This was particularly true of XX Corps that had been able to establish temporary contact with the Potsdam garrison. According to Wenck, no relief for Berlin by his army was now possible. This was even more so as support from the IX Army could no longer be expected.[240] Keitel gave Wenck permission to break off his attempt to relieve Berlin.[230]

At 04:00 hours on 29 April, in the *Führerbunker*, General Wilhelm Burgdorf, Goebbels, Krebs, and Bormann witnessed and signed the last will and testament of Adolf Hitler. Hitler dictated the document to Traudl Junge, shortly after he had married Eva Braun.[241,242]

After Rokossovsky's 2nd Belorussian Front had broken out of their bridgehead, General Gotthard Heinrici disobeyed Hitler's direct orders and allowed von Manteuffel's request for a general withdrawal of the III Panzer Army. By 29 April, Army Group Vistula Headquarters staff could no longer contact the IX Army, so there was little in the way of coordination that Heinrici's staff could still to do. As Heinrici had disobeyed a direct order from Hitler (in allowing von Manteuffel to retreat), he was relieved of his command. However, von Manteuffel refused Keitel's request that he take over, and although ordered to report to *Oberkommando der Wehrmacht* (OKW's or Armed Forces High Command) headquarters, Heinrici dallied and never arrived.[243] Keitel later recalled the incident in his memoirs and said that command passed to the senior army commander of the XXI Army, General Kurt von Tippelskirch.[244] Other sources claim that von Tippelskirch's appointment was temporary and only until the arrival of General Kurt Student,[245,246] but that Student was captured by the British and never arrived.[220] Whether von Tippelskirch or Student or both took command, the rapidly deteriorating situation that the Germans faced, meant that Army Group Vistula's coordination of the armies under its nominal command during the last few days of the war were of little significance.

In the early hours of 29 April, the 150th and 171st Rifle divisions started to fan out from the Moltke bridgehead into the surrounding streets and buildings. Initially the Soviets were unable to bring forward artillery, as the combat engineers had not had time to strengthen the bridge or build an alternative. The only form of heavy weaponry available to the assault troops were individual 'Katyusha' rockets lashed to short sections of railway lines. Major-General V. M. Shatilov's 150th Rifle Division had a particularly hard fight, capturing the heavily fortified Ministry of the Interior building. Lacking artillery, the men had to clear it room by room with grenades and sub-machine guns.[247]

In the south-east at dawn on 29 April, Colonel Antonov's 301st Rifle Division pressed on with its assault. After very heavy fighting, the formation managed to capture the Gestapo headquarters on Prinz-Albrecht-Strasse, but a *Waffen SS* counter-attack forced the regiments of the division to withdraw from the structure. Still confined to the building were seven inmates who had been spared in the massacre of other prisoners on 23 April.[234] To the south-west Chuikov's 8th Guards Army attacked north across the Landwehr canal into the Tiergarten.[248]

The *Nordland* Division was now under Mohnke's central command. All the men were exhausted from days and nights of continuous fighting. The Frenchmen of the *Nordland* had proved particularly good at destroying tanks, of the 108 Soviet tanks knocked out in the central district, they had accounted for about half of them. That afternoon the last two Knight's Crosses of the Third

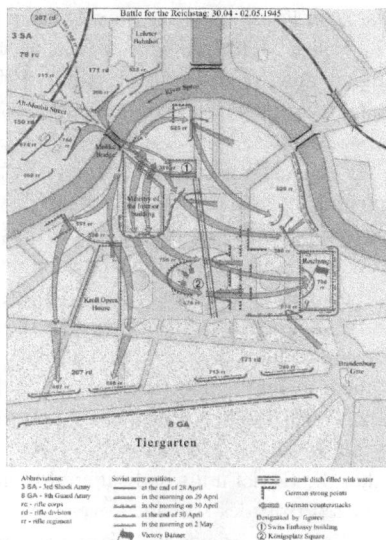

Figure 19: *Battle for the Reichstag*

Reich were awarded; one went to Frenchman Eugéne Vaulôt, who had per-
sonally destroyed eight tanks, the other was awarded to SS-*Sturmbannführer*
Friedrich Herzig, the commander of the 503 SS Heavy Panzer Battalion. Two
other men received less prestigious awards for only knocking out five tanks
each.[249]

During the evening of 29 April, at Weidling's headquarters in the
Bendlerblock, now within metres of the front line, Weidling discussed with
his divisional commanders, the possibility of breaking out to the south-west to
link up with the XII Army, whose spearhead had reached the village of Ferch
in Brandenburg on the banks of the Schwielowsee near Potsdam. The breakout
was planned to start the next night at 22:00.[249] Late in the evening, Krebs contacted General Alfred Jodl (Supreme Army Command) by radio: "Request im-
mediate report. Firstly of the whereabouts of Wenck's spearheads. Secondly
of time intended to attack. Thirdly of the location of the IX Army. Fourthly
of the precise place in which the IX Army will break through. Fifthly of the
whereabouts of General Rudolf Holste's spearhead."[240] In the early morning
of 30 April, Jodl replied to Krebs: "Firstly, Wenck's spearhead bogged down
south of Schwielow Lake. Secondly, XII Army therefore unable to continue
attack on Berlin. Thirdly, bulk of IX Army surrounded. Fourthly, Holste's
Corps on the defensive."[240,250,251,252]

By this time, several smaller Polish units had already taken part in the battle in Berlin (such as the 1st Polish Motorized Mortar Brigade, the 6th Polish Motorised Pontoon Battalion, and the 2nd Polish Howitzer Brigade)[253,254] Soviet forces were lacking infantry support, and armored units, without infantry support, were taking heavy casualties.[255,256] As of 30 April, the Soviet forces were joined by the Polish 1st Tadeusz Kościuszko Infantry Division after a request from the Soviet command for infantry reinforcements.[257,258] Originally, one infantry regiment was to support the 1st Mechanised Corps, and two, the 12th Guards Tank Corps; contrary to the original plan, two regiments (1st and 2nd) ended up supporting the 1st Corps, and only one (3rd) the 12th Corps.[259,260] The 3rd Polish Infantry Regiment was operating with the 66th Guards Tank Brigade of the 12th Guards Tank Corps.[255] The 1st Polish Infantry Regiment was split up into "combat teams" supporting the 19th and 35th Mechanized Brigades, with the 2nd Polish Infantry Regiment supporting the 219th Tank Brigade; all units of the Soviet 1st Mechanized Corps.[255] Upon arrival, the Polish forces found that the Soviet units had suffered tremendous losses; the 19th and 35th Mechanized Brigades sustained over 90% casualties, and thus the Polish 1st Infantry Regiment originally assigned to support them had to, in effect, take over their tasks.[255,261,262] The 66th Guards Tank Brigade of the 12th Corps that received the 3rd Polish Infantry Regiment for support had similarly taken heavy losses, having already lost 82 tanks due to insufficient infantry cover.[255,256]

Battle for the Reichstag

At 06:00 on 30 April the 150th Rifle Division had still not captured the upper floors of the Ministry of the Interior, but while the fighting was still going on, the 150th launched an attack from there across the 400 metres of Königsplatz towards the *Reichstag*. For the Soviets, the *Reichstag* was the symbol of the Third Reich (ironically, it was never restored by the Nazis after the fire); but it was of such significant value that the Soviets wanted to capture it before the May Day parade in Moscow. The assault was not an easy one. The Germans had dug a complicated network of trenches around the building and a collapsed tunnel had filled with water from the Spree forming a moat across Königsplatz. The initial infantry assault was decimated by cross fire from the *Reichstag* and the Kroll Opera House on the western side of Königsplatz. By now the Spree had been bridged and the Soviets were able to bring up tanks and artillery to support fresh assaults by the infantry, some of which were tasked with outflanking the Opera House and attacking it from the north-west. By 10:00 the soldiers of the 150th had reached the moat, but accurate fire from 12.8 cm guns, two kilometres away on the Berlin Zoo flak tower, prevented any further successful advance across the moat during daylight. Throughout the rest of the day, as ninety artillery pieces, some as large as the 203 mm howitzer, as well as *Katyusha* rocket launchers, bombarded the *Reichstag* and its defensive trenches. Colonel Negoda's 171st Rifle Division, on the left flank of the 150th, continued to capture the buildings of the diplomatic quarter to the north of Königsplatz.[263,264]

As the perimeter shrank and the surviving defenders fell back on the centre, they became concentrated. By now, there were about 10,000 soldiers in the city centre, who were being assaulted from all sides. One of the other main thrusts was along Wilhelmstrasse on which the Air Ministry, which was built of reinforced concrete, was situated. It was pounded by large concentrations of Soviet artillery. The remaining German Tiger tanks of the Hermann von Salza battalion took up positions in the east of the Tiergarten to defend the centre against the 3rd Shock Army (which, although heavily engaged around the *Reichstag*, was also flanking the area by advancing through the northern Tiergarten) and the 8th Guards Army advancing through the south of the Tiergarten. These Soviet forces had effectively cut the sausage-shaped area held by the Germans in half and made an escape to the west for those German troops in the centre much more difficult.[265]

During the morning, Mohnke informed Hitler the centre would be able to hold for less than two days. Later that morning, Weidling informed Hitler in person that the defenders would probably exhaust their ammunition that night and again asked Hitler permission to break out. At about 13:00, Weidling, who was back in his headquarters in the Bendlerblock, finally received Hitler's permission to attempt a breakout.[266] During the afternoon, Hitler shot himself and Braun took cyanide.[267,268] In accordance with Hitler's instructions, the bodies were burned in the garden of the Reich Chancellery.[269] In accordance with Hitler's last will and testament, Joseph Goebbels, the Minister for Public Enlightenment and Propaganda, became the new "Head of Government" and Chancellor of Germany (*Reichskanzler*). At 3:15 am, *Reichskanzler* Goebbels and Bormann sent a radio message to Admiral Karl Dönitz informing him of Hitler's death. Per Hitler's last wishes, Dönitz was appointed as the new "President of Germany" (*Reichspräsident*).

Starting from 16:00 on 30 April, the 1st Battalion of the Polish 1st Regiment (assigned to the region of 35th Mechanized Brigade) begun an assault on a barricade on Pestalozzistrasse, a major obstacle which made previous tank attacks in that direction suicidal.[270] The Polish 2nd and 3rd Regiments cleared the path through the barricades on Goethestrasse and Schillerstrasse for the tanks of the Soviet 19th Brigade.[271]

Because of the smoke, dusk came early to the centre of Berlin. At 18:00 hours, while Weidling and his staff finalized their breakout plans in the Bendlerblock, three regiments of the Soviet 150th Rifle Division, under cover of a heavy artillery barrage and closely supported by tanks, assaulted the *Reichstag*. All the

Figure 20: *Polish flag raised on the top of Berlin Victory Column on 2 May 1945*

windows were bricked up, but the soldiers managed to force the main doors and entered the main hall. The German garrison, of about 1,000 defenders (a mixture of sailors, SS and Hitler Youth) fired down on the Soviets from above, turning the main hall into a medieval style killing field. Suffering many casualties, the Soviets got beyond the main hall and started to work their way up through the building. The fire and subsequent wartime damage had turned the building's interior into a maze of rubble and debris amongst which the German defenders were strongly dug in.[272] The Soviet infantry were forced to clear them out. Fierce room-to-room fighting ensued.[273] As May Day approached Soviet troops reached the roof, but fighting continued inside. Moscow claimed that they hoisted the Red Flag on the top of the *Reichstag* at 22:50, however Beevor points out that this may have been an exaggeration as "Soviet propaganda was fixated with the idea of the *Reichstag* being captured by 1 May".[272] Whatever the truth, the fighting continued as there was still a large contingent of German soldiers down in the basement. The Germans were well stocked with food and ammunition and launched counter-attacks against the Red Army, leading to close fighting in and around the *Reichstag*.[273] Close combat raged throughout the night and the coming day of 1 May, until the evening when some German troops pulled out of the building and crossed the Friedrichstraße *S-Bahn* Station, where they moved into the ruins hours before the main breakout across the Spree.[274] About 300 of the last German combatants surrendered.[272] A further 200 defenders were dead and another 500 were already *hors de combat*, lying wounded in the basement, many before the final assault had started.[272]

Capture of Charlottenburg

The barricade at Pestalozzistrasse was taken on the morning of 1 May, allowing Soviet tanks of the 34th Brigade to advance and to reestablish contact with the 19th Mechanized Brigade supported by the 2nd and 3rd Battalion of the 1st Regiment, which pushed through the barricades at Goethestrasse and Schillerstrasse.[270] Further, heavily fortified German positions in and around the church at the Karl August-Platz were taken, allowing the Polish and Soviet units to advance along the Goethestrasse and Schillerstrasse.[271] In the meantime, the Polish 2nd Regiment, with its own artillery support, took the heavily fortified Berlin Institute of Technology that was situated in the triangle between Charlottenburgerstrasse, Hardenbergstrasse and Jebenstrasse.[275,276] With support by the Polish 3rd Infantry Regiment, the Soviet 66th Guards Tank Brigade (which had only 15 tanks) broke through Franklinstrasse and advanced towards the Berlin-Tiergarten station.[277] The stronghold of the Tiergarten (*S-Bahn*) station was then secured by the 3rd Infantry Regiment.[278] Thereafter, Polish and Soviet units took control of the Zoologischer Garten station and the railway line between them. By these actions, the Red Army had broken through the central Berlin west line of defence.[279]

End of the battle

At about 04:00 on 1 May, Krebs talked to Chuikov, commander of the Soviet 8th Guards Army.[280] Krebs returned empty-handed after refusing to agree to an unconditional surrender. Only *Reichskanzler* Goebbels now had the authority to agree to an unconditional surrender. In the late afternoon, Goebbels had his children poisoned. At about 20:00, Goebbels and his wife, Magda, left the bunker and close to the entrance bit on a cyanide ampoule, and either shot themselves at the same time or were given a *coup de grâce* immediately afterwards by the SS guard detailed to dispose of their bodies.[281] As promised by the Soviets, at 10:45 on 1 May they unleashed a "hurricane of fire" on the German pocket in the centre to force the Germans to surrender unconditionally.[265]

For a brief period after Hitler's suicide, Goebbels was Germany's *Reichskanzler*. On 1 May, after Goebbels' own suicide, for an equally brief period, *Reichspräsident* Admiral Karl Dönitz appointed Ludwig von Krosigk as *Reichskanzler*. The headquarters of the Dönitz government were located around Flensburg, along with Mürwik, near the Danish border. Accordingly, the Dönitz administration was referred to as the Flensburg government.

Figure 21: *Weidendammer bridge in 2006*

The commanders of two formidable Berlin fortresses agreed to surrender to the Soviets, so sparing both sides the losses involved in further bombardment and assault. The commander of the Zoo flak tower (that had proved impervious to direct hits from 203 mm howitzer shells) was asked to surrender on 30 April; after a long delay a message was sent back to the Soviets on 1 May informing them that the garrison would surrender to the Soviets at midnight that night. The reason for the delay was because the garrison intended to join in the attempt at a breakout. The other fortress was the Spandau Citadel of *Trace italienne* design which although several hundred years old presented a difficult structure to storm. After negotiations, the citadel's commander surrendered to Lieutenant-General F. I. Perkhorovitch's 47th Army just after 15:00 on 1 May.[282]

Breakout

Weidling had given the order for the survivors to break out to the northwest starting at around 21:00 hours on 1 May.[283] The breakout started later than planned at around 23:00 hours. The first group from the Reich Chancellery was led by Mohnke. Bormann, Werner Naumann, and remaining *Führerbunker* personnel followed. Burgdorf, who played a key role in the death of Erwin Rommel, along with Krebs, committed suicide.[240] Mohnke's group avoided the Weidendammer Bridge (over which the mass breakout took

Figure 22: *Charlotten bridge. Rebuilt in 1926, it survived World War II.*

place) and crossed by a footbridge, but his group became split. A Tiger tank that spearheaded the first attempt to storm the Weidendammer Bridge was destroyed.[284,285] There followed two more attempts and on the third attempt, made around 1:00, Martin Bormann and SS doctor Ludwig Stumpfegger in another group from the Reich Chancellery managed to cross the Spree. They were reported to have died a short distance from the bridge, their bodies seen and identified by Arthur Axmann who followed the same route.[286,287]

Krukenberg and many of the survivors of the remnants of the *Nordland* Division crossed the Spree shortly before dawn but could not break through and were forced back into the centre. There they split up; some discarded their uniforms and tried to pass themselves off as civilians, but most were either killed or, like Krukenberg, captured.[288] An attempt to break out northward along the Schönhauser Allee by German troops on the north-eastern side of the central defence area failed because the Soviets were now aware that breakout attempts were being made and were hurriedly putting cordons in place to stop them. The remnants of the *Münchenberg* Division (five tanks, four artillery pieces, and a handful of troops[289]) and the remnants of the 18th Panzer Grenadier and 9th Parachute divisions broke out of the centre westward through the Tiergarten. They were followed by thousands of stragglers and civilians.[290] Spandau was still in the hands of a Hitler Youth detachment, so an attempt was made to force a passage across the Charlottenbrücke (Charlotten bridge) over the Havel. Despite heavy shelling which killed many, German weight of numbers meant that they were able to drive the Soviet infantry back and many thousands crossed into Spandau. The armoured vehicles that crossed the bridge made for Staaken.[291]

Mohnke (and what was left of his group) could not break through the Soviet rings. Most were taken prisoner and some committed suicide. General Mohnke and the others who had been in the *Führerbunker* were interrogated by SMERSH.[292] Only a handful of survivors reached the Elbe and surrendered to the Western Allies. The majority were killed or captured by the Soviets. The number of German soldiers and civilians killed attempting the breakout is unknown.[293]

Capitulation

On the morning of 2 May, the Soviets stormed the Reich Chancellery. In the official Soviet version, the battle was similar to that of the battle for the *Reichstag*. There was an assault over Wilhelmplatz and into the building with a howitzer to blast open the front doors and several battles within the building. Major Anna Nikulina, a political officer with Lieutenant-General I. P. Rossly's 9th Rifle Corps of the 5th Shock Army carried and unfurled the red flag on the roof. However, Beevor suggests that the official Soviet description is probably an exaggeration, as most of the German combat troops had left in the breakouts the night before, resistance must have been far less than that inside the *Reichstag*.[294]

At 01:00 hours, the Soviets picked up radio message from the German LVI Corps requesting a cease-fire and stating that emissaries would come under a white flag to Potsdamer bridge. General Weidling surrendered with his staff at 06:00 hours. He was taken to see Lieutenant-General Chuikov at 8:23 am. Chuikov, who had commanded the successful defence of Stalingrad, asked: "You are the commander of the Berlin garrison?" Weidling replied: "Yes, I am the commander of the LVI Panzer Corps." Chuikov then asked: "Where is Krebs? What did he say?" Weidling replied: "I saw him yesterday in the Reich Chancellery." Weidling then added: "I thought he would commit suicide."[240] In the discussions that followed, Weidling agreed to an unconditional surrender of the city of Berlin. He agreed to order the city's defenders to surrender to the Soviets. Under the direction of Chuikov and Soviet General Vasily Sokolovsky (Chief of staff of the 1st Ukrainian Front), Weidling put his order to surrender in writing.[240,295]

The 350-strong garrison of the Zoo flak tower finally left the building. There was sporadic fighting in a few isolated buildings where some SS still refused to surrender. The Soviets simply blasted any such building to rubble. Most Germans, soldiers and civilians, were grateful to receive food issued at Red

Army soup kitchens. The Soviets went house to house and rounded up anyone in a uniform including firemen and railwaymen, a total of 180,000 and marched them eastwards as prisoners of war.[296]

Aftermath

The Red Army made a major effort to feed the residents of the city which began on Colonel-General Nikolai Berzarin's orders.[297] However, in many areas, vengeful Soviet troops (usually rear echelon units) looted, raped (an estimated 100,000) and murdered civilians for several weeks.[298]

Notes

Bibliography

- Antill, Peter (2005). *Berlin 1945: End of the Thousand Year Reich*. Campaign Series. **159** (illustrated ed.). Oxford: Osprey Publishing. p. 85[299]. ISBN 978-1-84176-915-8.
- Beevor, Antony (2002). *Berlin: The Downfall 1945*. London; New York: Viking-Penguin Books. ISBN 978-0-670-03041-5.
- Beevor, Antony (2012). *The Second World War* (illustrated ed.). UK: Hachette. ISBN 9780297860709.
- Dollinger, Hans (1997). *The Decline and Fall of Nazi Germany and Imperial Japan* (reprint ed.). New York: Crown Publishers. ISBN 978-0-7537-0009-9.
- Fischer, Thomas (2008). *Soldiers of the Leibstandarte*. Winnipeg: J.J. Fedorowicz Publishing. ISBN 978-0-921991-91-5.
- Hamilton, Stephan (2008). *Bloody Streets: The Soviet Assault on Berlin, April 1945*. Solihull: Helion & Co. ISBN 978-1-906033-12-5.
- Joachimsthaler, Anton (1999) [1995]. *The Last Days of Hitler: The Legends, The Evidence, The Truth*. London: Brockhampton Press. ISBN 978-1-86019-902-8.
- Kershaw, Ian (2008). *Hitler: A Biography*. W. W. Norton & Company Publishing. ISBN 0-393-06757-2.
- Kiederling, Gerhard (1987). *Berlin 1945–1986. Geschichte der Hauptstadt der DDR*. Berlin: Dietz Verlag. ISBN 978-3-320-00774-4.
- Komornicki, Stanisław (1967). *Poles in the Battle of Berlin*[300]. Ministry of National Defense Pub. OCLC 5297730[301].
- Ladd, Brian (1998). *The Ghosts of Berlin: Confronting German History in the Urban Landscape* (illustrated ed.). University of Chicago Press. p. 99[302]–102. ISBN 978-0-226-46762-7.

- Le Tissier, Tony (2010) [1999]. *Race for the Reichstag: The 1945 Battle for Berlin.* Pen and Sword. ISBN 978-1-84884-230-4.
- McDonnald, Alexander Hopkins, ed. (1951). *The Encyclopedia Americana.* **6.** Americana Corporation. p. 720.
- Mende, Hans-Jürgen; Wernicke, Kurt; Chod, Kathrin; Schwenk, Herbert; Weißpflug, Hainer (2001). *Berlin Mitte: Das Lexikon.* Berlin: Stapp. ISBN 978-3-87776-111-3.
- MI5 staff (8 June 2012). "Hitler's last days: Hitler's will and marriage"[303]. Retrieved 1 May 2013.
- Prakash, Gyan; Kruse, Kevin Michael (2008). *The spaces of the modern city: imaginaries, politics, and everyday life* (illustrated ed.). Princeton University Press. pp. 44[304]–46. ISBN 978-0-691-13343-0.
- Siepen, Edith (2011). *Peeps at Great Cities – Berlin.* BoD – Books on Demand. p. 7[305]. ISBN 978-3-86403-134-2.
- Tiemann, Ralf (1998). *The Leibstandarte IV/2.* Winnipeg: J.J. Fedorowicz Publishing. ISBN 978-0-921991-40-3.
- Urban Land Institute (2006). *Urban land.* **65.** Urban Land Institute. p. 88.
- Ziemke, Earl F. (1969). *Battle For Berlin: End Of The Third Reich.* NY:Ballantine Books: Macdonald & Co: London. ISBN 978-0-356-02960-3.
- Zbiniewicz, Fryderyk (1988). *Armia Radziecka w wojnie z hitlerowskimi Niemcami 1941–1945.* Warsaw: Wydawnictwo Ministerstwa Obrony. ISBN 978-83-11-07489-7.

Further reading

| | Wikimedia Commons has media related to *Battle in Berlin*. |

| | Wikimedia Commons has media related to *Battle of Berlin*. |

- Antill, P, *Battle for Berlin: April – May 1945 (website)*, Appendix 1: Soviet Order of Battle for the Battle for Berlin[306] and Appendix 2: German Order of Battle for Operation Berlin[307]), cites Le Tissier, T (1988), *The Battle of Berlin 1945*, London: Jonathan Cape, pp. 196–207; 208–214
- Hastings, Max (2004), *Armageddon: The Battle for Germany, 1944–1945*, Macmillan, ISBN 978-0-333-90836-5
- Hill, Alexander (2017), *The Red Army and the Second World War*, Cambridge University Press, ISBN 978-1-1070-2079-5.

- Hillers, Marta, *A Woman in Berlin: Six Weeks in the Conquered City*, translated by Bell, Anthes, ISBN 978-0-8050-7540-3
- Krivosheev, G. F. (1997), *Soviet Casualties and Combat Losses in the Twentieth Century*, London: Greenhill Books, ISBN 978-1-85367-280-4
- Le Tissier, Tony (2010), *Charlemagne – The 33rd Waffen-SS Grenadier Division of the SS*, Pen & Sword, ISBN 978-1-84884-231-1
- Naimark, Norman M. (1995), *The Russians in Germany: A History of the Soviet Zone of Occupation, 1945–1949*, Cambridge: Belknap, ISBN 978-0-674-78405-5
- Read, Anthony (1993), *The Fall of Berlin*, London: Pimlico, ISBN 978-0-7126-0695-0
- Remme, Tilman, *The Battle for Berlin in World War Two*[308], BBC
- Ryan, Cornelius, *The Last Battle*, ISBN 978-0-684-80329-6
- Sanders, Ian J., *Photos of World War 2 Berlin Locations today*[309], archived from the original[310] on 26 October 2009
- Shepardson, Donald E. (1998), "The Fall of Berlin and the Rise of a Myth", *The Journal of Military History*, **62** (1): 135–153, doi: 10.2307/120398[311]
- White, Osmar, *By the eyes of a war correspondent*[312], archived from the original[313] on 18 March 2007 Alternative account of crimes against civilians

Battle for the Reichstag

Raising a Flag over the Reichstag

Raising a Flag over the Reichstag is a historic World War II photograph, taken during the Battle of Berlin on 2 May 1945. It shows Meliton Kantaria and Mikhail Yegorov raising the flag of the Soviet Union atop the Reichstag building. The photograph was reprinted in thousands of publications and came to be regarded around the world as one of the most significant and recognizable images of World War II. Owing to the secrecy of Soviet media, the identities of the men in the picture were often disputed, as was that of the photographer, Yevgeny Khaldei, who was identified only after the fall of the Soviet Union. It became a symbol of the Soviet victory over Nazi Germany.

Background

The Battle of Berlin was the final major offensive of the European Theatre of World War II and was designated the Berlin Strategic Offensive Operation by the Soviet Union. Starting on 16 April 1945, the Red Army breached the German front as a result of the Vistula–Oder Offensive and rapidly advanced westward through Germany, as fast as 30–40 kilometres a day. The battle for Berlin lasted from late 20 April 1945 until 2 May and was one of the bloodiest in history.

Erected in 1894, the Reichstag's architecture was magnificent for its time. The building contributed much to German history and was considered by the Red Army to be the symbol of their fascist enemy. However, to the Nazis, the Reichstag was a symbol of democracy and representative government; consequently they had left it closed and damaged since the infamous Reichstag fire in 1933. Instead of being a center of fascist power, the Reichstag had been

closed down for 12 years, essentially the entirety of the Nazi reign, with subsequent meetings of the Reichstag convening at the nearby Kroll Opera House
instead. After fierce combat within its walls, the Soviets finally captured the
Reichstag on 2 May 1945.

Taking the photograph

The Reichstag was seen as symbolic of, and at the heart of, Nazi Germany. It
was arguably the most symbolic target in Berlin. The events surrounding the
flag-raising are murky due to the confusion of the fight at the building. On 30
April there was great pressure from Stalin to take the building, in time for the
International Workers' Day, 1 May.[314]Wikipedia:Accuracy dispute#Disputed
statement Initially, two planes dropped several large red banners on the roof
that appeared to have caught on the bombed-out dome. Additionally, a number
of reports had reached headquarters that two parties, M. M. Bondar from the
380th Rifle Regiment and Captain V. N. Makov of the 756th might have been
able to hoist a flag during the day of 30 April.[315] These reports were received
by Marshal G. K. Zhukov, who issued an announcement stating that his troops
had captured the Reichstag and hoisted a flag. However, when correspondents
arrived, they found no Soviets in the building, but rather they were pinned
down outside by German fire. After fierce fighting both outside and inside
the building, a flag was raised at 22:40 on 30 April 1945, when 23-year-old
Rakhimzhan Qoshqarbaev climbed the building and inserted a flag into the
crown of the mounted female statue of "Germania", symbolizing Germany.
As this happened at night, it was too dark to take a photograph.[316] The next
day the flag was taken down by the Germans.[316] The Red Army finally gained
control of the entire building on 2 May.[317]

The original photo (top) was altered (bottom) by editing the watch on
Yegorov's right wrist[318]

On 2 May 1945, Khaldei scaled the now pacified Reichstag to take his picture.
He was carrying with him a large flag, sewn from three tablecloths for this very
purpose, by his uncle.[319] The official story would later be that two hand-picked
soldiers, Meliton Kantaria (Georgian) and Mikhail Yegorov (Russian), raised
the Soviet flag over the Reichstag,[314,320,321,322] and the photograph would often
be used as depicting the event. Some authors state that for political reasons the
subjects of the photograph were changed and the actual man to hoist the flag
was Alexei Kovalyov,[323,324] (also known as Alyosha Kovalyov) a Ukrainian,
who was told by the NKVD to keep quiet about it.[323]

However, according to Khaldei himself, when he arrived at the Reichstag, he simply asked the soldiers who happened to be passing by to help with the staging of the photoshoot; there were only four of them, including Khaldei, on the roof: the one who was attaching the flag was 18-year-old Private Alexei Kovalyov from Kiev, the two others were Abdulkhakim Ismailov from Dagestan and Leonid Gorychev (also mentioned as Aleksei Goryachev) from Minsk. The photograph was taken with a Leica III rangefinder camera with a 35mm f3.5 lens.

Aftermath

The photo was published 13 May 1945 in the *Ogonyok* magazine.[318] While many photographers took pictures of flags on the roof, it was Khaldei's image that stuck.[318]

Censorship

After taking the symbolic photo, Khaldei quickly returned to Moscow. He further edited the image at the request of the editor-in-chief of the *Ogonyok*, who noticed that Senior Sergeant Abdulkhakim Ismailov, who is supporting the flag-bearer, was wearing two watches, which could imply he had looted one of them, an action punishable by execution.[318] Using a needle, Khaldei was able to remove the watch from the right wrist.[325,318] He also added to the smoke in the background, copying it from another picture to make the scene more dramatic.[326]

Bibliography

Notes

References

<templatestyles src="Template:Refbegin/styles.css" />

- Adams, Simon (2008). *The Eastern Front* (2008 ed.). The Rosen Publishing Group. ISBN 1-4042-1862-9. – Total pages: 48
- Antill, Peter; Dennis, Peter (2005). *Berlin 1945: End of the Thousand Year Reich* (when ed.). Osprey Publishing. ISBN 1-84176-915-0. – Total pages: 96
- Baumann, Von Doc (2010-01-03). "Dramatische Rauchwolcken"[327] (in German). Der Spiegel. Retrieved 2011-06-03.
- Beevor, Antony (2003). *Berlin: The Downfall 1945*. London: Penguin Books. ISBN 978-0-14-028696-0.

Figure 23: *An Azerbaijani stamp commemorating the
65th anniversary of victory in the Great Patriotic War.*

- Broekmeyer, M. J. (2004). *Stalin, the Russians, and their war: 1941-
  1945* (2004 ed.). University of Wisconsin Press. ISBN 0-299-19594-5. –
  Total pages: 315
- Conquest, Robert (1991). *The Great Terror: A Reassessment* (1991 ed.).
  Oxford University Press US. ISBN 0-19-507132-8. – Total pages: 584
- Dallas, Gregor (2006). *1945: The War That Never Ended* (2006 ed.).
  Yale University Press. ISBN 0-300-11988-7. – Total pages: 792
- Lenin, Vladimir (1929). *Collected Works, Volume XX* (1929 ed.). Inter-
  national Publishers. ISBN 1-4179-1577-3.
- Lindemann, Albert S. (2000). *Esau's Tears: Modern anti-semitism and
  the rise of the Jews* (2000 ed.). Cambridge University Press. ISBN 0-521-
  79538-9. – Total pages: 568
- Lucas, Dean (2010-02-28). "Flag on the Reichstag"[328]. FamousPic-
  tures.org. Retrieved 2013-05-03.
- Sontheimer, Michael (2008-07-05). "The Art of Soviet Propaganda:
  Iconic Red Army Reichstag Photo Faked"[329]. Der Spiegel. Retrieved
  2011-06-03.
- Tissier, Tony Le (1999). *Race for the Reichstag: the 1945 Battle for
  Berlin* (1999 ed.). Routledge. ISBN 0-7146-4929-5. – Total pages: 265

- Walkowitz, Daniel J.; Knauer, Lisa Maya (2004). *Memory and the impact of political transformation in public space Radical perspectives* (when ed.). Duke University Press. ISBN 0-8223-3364-3. – Total pages: 326
- "За него Геринг получил по шее"[330] ["Göring received a neckslap because of that man". Interview with Anna Haldey]. *Interview* (in Russian). Nizhny Novgorod: Moskovskij Komsomolets. 2010-05-12. Retrieved 2011-06-03.Wikipedia:Link rot
- "Iconic WWII photo honored at Berlin exhibit"[331]. *Associated Press*. USA Today. 2008-06-15. Retrieved 2012-05-20.
- "Iconic WWII photo staged"[332]. *Associated Press*. USA Today. 2008-06-16. Retrieved 2012-05-20.
- "The Art of Soviet Propaganda Iconic Red Army Reichstag Photo Faked - SPIEGEL ONLINE"[329]. Spiegel. 2008-05-07. Retrieved 2012-05-20.
- "Muere el último sobreviviente de la foto más famosa del fin de la II Guerra"[333] (in Spanish). La Tercera. 2010-02-18. Retrieved 2012-05-20.
- "Soviet soldier pictured in iconic 1945 Reichstag photo dies"[334]. *Associated Press*. The Guardian. 2010-02-17. Retrieved 2012-05-20.

Battle Outside Berlin

Battle of Halbe

Battle of Halbe	
Part of World War II	

Destroyed German Army vehicles near Spree Forest during the Battle of Halbe

Date	April 24 – May 1, 1945
Location	Halbe, Germany
	52°6′24"N 13°42′3"E[335] Coordinates: 52°6′24"N 13°42′3"E[335]
Result	Soviet victory

Belligerents	
🏴 Germany	🚩 Soviet Union

Commanders and leaders	
Theodor Busse Walther Wenck	Georgy Zhukov Ivan Konev

Strength	
210,000	280,000

Casualties and losses	
• Over 35,000Wikipedia:Citation needed - 60,000 killed and 120,000 captured (25,000 escaped from pocket) • 10,000 civilians killed	Less than 20,000 killed-Wikipedia:Citation needed

The **Battle of Halbe** (German: *Kessel von Halbe*, Russian: Хальбский котёл, Halbe pocket) from April 24 – May 1, 1945[336] was a battle in which the

German Ninth Army, under the command of General Theodor Busse, was destroyed as a fighting force by the Red Army during the Battle for Berlin.

The Ninth Army, encircled in a large pocket in the Spree Forest region southeast of Berlin, attempted to break out westwards through the village of Halbe and the pine forests south of Berlin to link up with the German Twelfth Army commanded by General Walther Wenck with the intention of heading west and surrendering to the Western Allies. To do this, the Ninth Army had to fight their way through three lines of Soviet troops of the 1st Ukrainian Front under the command of Marshal Ivan Konev, while at the same time units of the 1st Belorussian Front, under the command of Marshal Georgy Zhukov, attacked the German rearguard from the northeast.

After heavy fighting, about 30,000 German soldiers—one fifth of those originally in the pocket—reached the comparative safety of the Twelfth Army's front lines. The rest were either killed or captured by Soviet forces.Wikipedia:Citation needed

Prelude

On April 16, the Red Army started the Battle of Berlin with a three Front attack across the Oder-Neisse line. By April 21, they had broken through the German front line in two places and had started to surround Berlin. The German Ninth Army covered the defenses of the Seelow Heights against Marshal Zhukov's 1st Belorussian Front, but its position was unhinged by the successful attack of Marshal Ivan Konev's 1st Ukrainian Front (against Army Group Centre) on the Neisse. By April 20, the Ninth Army retreated south-east of Berlin, opening the way for the 1st Belorussian Front.[337]

Because of the high speed of the advance of Konev's forces, the Ninth Army was now threatened with envelopment by the two Soviet pincers that were heading for Berlin from the south and east. The southern pincer consisted of the 3rd and 4th Guards Tank Armies which had penetrated the furthest and had already cut through the area behind the Ninth Army's front lines.[337]

Figure 24: *Generaloberst Theodor Busse (standing, far right) in a meeting with Adolf Hitler, March 1945*

Encirclement

German dispositions

The command of the V SS Mountain Corps, encircled with the Ninth Army north of Forst, passed from the 4th Panzer Army (part of Army Group Centre) to the Ninth Army (part of Army Group Vistula under the command of General Gotthard Heinrici). The corps was still holding on to Cottbus. While the bulk of Army Group Centre was being forced, by the advance of the 1st Ukrainian Front, to retreat along its lines of communication to the south-west towards Czechoslovakia, the southern flank of the 4th Panzer Army had some local successes counterattacking north against the 1st Ukrainian Front.

Contrary to realities on the ground, Hitler ordered the Ninth Army to hold Cottbus and set up a front facing west, then they were to attack into the Soviet columns advancing north. This would allow them to form the northern pincer which would meet with the 4th Panzer Army coming from the south and en-velop the 1st Ukrainian Front before destroying it. They were to anticipate an attack south by the 3rd Panzer Army and to be ready to be the southern arm of a pincer attack which would envelop the 1st Belorussian Front, which would then be destroyed by SS-general Felix Steiner's III SS Panzer Corps advancing from the north of Berlin. Later in the day, Steiner made it plain that he did not have the divisions to make this effort. Heinrici then explained to Hitler's staff that unless the Ninth Army retreated immediately, it would be enveloped by the Soviet forces. He stressed it was already too late for the unit to move north-west to Berlin and would have to retreat west.

At his afternoon situation conference on April 22, Hitler fell into a rage when he realised that his plans of the day before were not going to be implemented. He declared that the war was lost, blamed the generals and announced that he would stay in Berlin until the end and then kill himself. In an attempt to coax Hitler out of his rage, the Chief of Staff of the OKW, General Alfred Jodl, speculated that the Twelfth Army, which was facing the American forces, could move to Berlin because the Americans already on the Elbe River were unlikely to move further east. Hitler immediately seized upon the idea and within hours, the army's commander, General Walther Wenck, was ordered to disengage from the American forces and move the Twelfth Army north-east to support Berlin. It was then realised that if the Ninth Army moved west, it could link up with the Twelfth Army. In the evening, Heinrici was given permission to make the linkup.

Although in Hitler's mindWikipedia:Citation needed the Twelfth Army was going to break through to Berlin, and the Ninth Army, once it had broken through to the Twelfth Army, was going to help them, there is no evidence that Generals Heinrici, Busse or Wenck thought that this was at all possible. However, Hitler's agreement to allow the Ninth Army to break through to the Twelfth Army would allow a window through which sizable numbers of German troops could retreat to the west and surrender to the American forces, which is exactly what Wenck and Busse agreed to do. This was made easier when, shortly after midnight on April 25, Busse was given authority "to decide for himself the best direction of attack".[338]

The situation of the Ninth Army

Before being encircled, the Ninth Army had already suffered heavy losses in the Battle of the Seelow Heights. It is estimated that, at the start of the encirclement, it had fewer than 1,000 guns and mortars, approximately 79 tanks, and probably a total of 150–200 combat-ready armoured fighting vehicles left. In all, there were about 80,000 men in the pocket, the majority of whom belonged to the Ninth Army, consisting of the XI SS Panzer Corps, V SS Mountain Corps and the newly acquired V Corps, but there was also the Frankfurt Garrison.[339] The number of tanks reported included 36 tanks in the XI SS Panzer Corps, including up to 14 King Tigers of the 102nd SS Heavy Panzer Battalion. Air supply was attempted on April 25 and 26, but could not be carried out because the planes that had taken off could not find the drop point for supply, and no contact with the encircled army could be established.

Figure 25: *Barracks ruins in Kummersdorf Gut in Brandenburg*

The pocket into which the Ninth Army had been pushed by troops of the 1st Belorussian and 1st Ukrainian Fronts was a region of lakes and forest in the Spree Forest south-east of Fürstenwalde. The Soviet forces, having broken through and surrounded their primary objective of Berlin, then turned to mopping up those forces in the pocket. On the afternoon of April 25, the Soviet 3rd, 33rd and 69th Armies, as well as the 2nd Guards Cavalry Corps (which was a formation capable of infiltration through difficult terrain such as forests), attacked the pocket from the north-east as ordered by Marshal Georgy Zhukov, the commander of the 1st Belorussian Front. Konev knew that to break out to the west, the Ninth Army would have to cross the Berlin–Dresden Autobahn south of a chain of lakes starting at Teupitz and running north-east. On the same day of his attack in the north-east, Zhukov sent the 3rd Guards Army to support the 28th Army, which was ready to close the likely breakout route over the Berlin–Dresden Autobahn.

Soviet dispositions

Soviet forces ordered to attack the Ninth Army numbered around 280,000 men, 7,400 guns and mortars, 280 tanks and self-propelled guns, and 1,500 aircraft. The force included six Air Corps and the 1st Guards Breakthrough Artillery Division, which was committed on April 25.[340]

In the area to the west of the encirclement, Soviet forces were already positioned in depth, with (from the north)

- the 28th Army's 128th Rifle Corps in the area of Mittenwalde and Motzen;

  the 3rd Guards Rifle Corps in the area of Tornow, Radeland, Baruth/Mark, Golssen;

- the 3rd Guards Army's 120th Rifle Corps south of Halbe;

  the 21st Rifle Corps along the Berlin to Dresden Autobahn 13 to the west of Lübben;

- the 13th Army's 102nd Rifle Corps with the 117th Guards Rifle Division near Luckenwalde,

  the 27th Rifle Corps's 280th Rifle Division at Jüterbog, where the Wehrmacht's main artillery school was located.

In terms of mechanized formations, the 3rd Guards Tank Army's 9th Mechanised Corps had its 71st Mechanized Brigade between Teupitz and Neuhof; the 4th Guards Tank Army's 68th Guards Tank Brigade stood near Kummersdorf Gut; and the 3rd Guards Army's 25th Tank Corps near Duben. Both the 3rd Guards Army and the 13th Army were to be heavily reinforced throughout the battle, as they were to be in the path of the German break-out. A reinforcement of particular note was the deployment of the 1st Guards Breakthrough Artillery Division under the command of the 3rd Guards Army in the sector of Teurow to Briesen.[341,342]

Breakout

The Twelfth Army's attack and the Ninth Army's plan

The relief attempt by the Twelfth Army started on April 24 with General Wenck's XX Corps attacking east and northwards. During the night, the *Theodor Körner RAD Division* attacked the Soviet 5th Guards Mechanised Corps, under the command of General I. P. Yermakov, near Treuenbrietzen. The next day, the *Scharnhorst* Division started to engage the Soviet troops in and around Beelitz and caught the 4th Guards Tank Army's 6th Guards Mechanized Corps' open flank, overrunning rear-area units. While the *Ulrich von Hutten* Division tried to reach Potsdam, with the *Scharnhorst* Division on its eastern flank, to open a corridor into Berlin, other elements of the Twelfth Army, as Wenck had agreed with Busse, pushed east to meet the Ninth Army.

In the words of Busse to Wenck, the Ninth Army was planning to push west "like a caterpillar". According to General Busse's plan, the heavy King Tiger tanks of the 502nd SS Heavy Panzer Battalion should lead this caterpillar. The metaphor is quite apt because, as the head led the way, the rear-guard in the tail was going to be engaged in just as heavy fighting trying to disengage from following Soviet forces.[338]

On the night of April 25/26, a new order was issued to the Ninth and Twelfth Armies by Hitler. It stipulated that:

- The Twelfth Army was to cut off the 4th Guards Tank Army by reaching the line Beelitz to Ferch, and to attack eastwards to unite with the Ninth Army.
- The Ninth Army was to hold on to its eastern front between Spreewald and Fürstenwalde, and to attack westward to link up with the Twelfth Army.
- Once both armies were combined, they were to attack northwards and open a corridor through the Red Army's encirclement of Berlin.[343]

The final army conference of the Ninth Army took place at 1500 hours on April 28. At this point, contact was lost with the V Corps and the V SS Mountain Corps. The conference found that the only possible break-out route had to lead through Halbe. This was not difficult for the Soviet commanders to deduce as well, while, on the other hand, Ninth Army had virtually no information about the Soviet force dispositions between it and the Twelfth Army. From this conference onward, command and control within the Ninth Army collapsed. There was almost no contact between the Ninth Army headquarters and Army Group Vistula, and little contact with formations under Ninth Army command. There were few or no maps to guide planning or combat operations.

In his book *Slaughter at Halbe*, Tony Le Tissier accused General Busse of failing to exercise effective command and control of the encircled army, thereby contributing to the failure of successive break-out attempts. Le Tissier writes that Busse's initial movement of his HQ put him into a situation where he lost the ability to control the formations in the pocket, and in his break-out plan, Ninth Army HQ was to be placed immediately behind the spearhead of the breakout, the 502nd SS Heavy Tank Battalion, which effectively reduced his ability to exercise command to the tactical level. He also accuses Busse of failing to adequately support the first breakout attempt (see below). The spearhead for the Ninth Army break-out plan on April 28 was to be the 502nd SS Heavy Panzer Battalion with remaining elements of the Panzergrenadier Division Kurmark. These units were split into two wedges. The northern wedge included the 502nd SS Panzer, Ninth Army HQ, XI SS Panzer Corps HQ, and Panzergrenadier Division Kurmark HQ. Remnants of the 21st Panzer Division were to cover in a north-westerly direction, while remnants of the 32nd SS Division *30. Januar* was to cover the east and provide the rearguard.[344]

The first breakout attempt

On the evening of April 25, Busse ordered the two battlegroups - *Kampfgruppe von Luck*, consisting of the 21st Panzer Division and *Kampfgruppe Pipkorn*, containing the 35th SS and Police Grenadier Division, both named after their commanders - to attempt a break-out in the direction of the road centre of Baruth to obtain the use of roads to Luckenwalde and Jüterbog. *Von Luck*, consisting mainly of the 125th Panzer Grenadier Regiment and tanks from the 22nd Panzer Regiment, started from Halbe, while *Pipkorn*, made up from the remains of the 35th SS Division with tanks from the 10th SS Panzer Division, started from Schleepitz. Colonel von Luck's orders were to open a corridor and keep it open for the sole use of military units of the Ninth Army. No civilians were to be allowed to use it. *Von Luck* made good progress across the Berlin–Dresden Autobahn until it hit the Soviet defenses of the 50th Guards Rifle Division at Baruth, which had been reinforced by dug-in Stalin tanks. *Pipkorn* ran into the defenses of 329th Rifle Division early on, and the battle group was scattered, with some armoured elements, including Panther tanks, reaching Baruth. A pitched battle developed at Baruth, which was impossible for the German battlegroups to win. Busse ordered Luck to stay near Baruth, but discontinue the attack when informed of this. However, Luck disobeyed the order and disbanded his battle group, allowing soldiers to try to attempt to breakout individually.Wikipedia:Citation needed

On the following day, the battle continued around Baruth, and tank-hunting teams blew up some of the dug-in Soviet tanks. Some supply canisters were delivered by air, but the strength of the battle group was insufficient to hold off a Soviet counter-attack. Heavy air attacks, a strike by the 4th Bomber Air Corps around noon with 55 aircraft, and repeated strikes by the 1st and 2nd Air Assault Corps with 8–10 aircraft each, a total of ca. 500 missions, caused heavy casualties and chaos. The forces of the two battle groups were destroyed, with Soviet reports claiming 5,000 prisoners taken, 40 tanks and self-propelled guns destroyed, and almost 200 guns and mortars captured.[345] These forces and weapons were sorely missed during later break-out attempts. Pipkorn, the commander of the other battle group, was killed during the battle, and Luck taken prisoner on April 27. Few of the survivors of the battle reached the Elbe.[346]

The second breakout attempt

The next morning, the German vanguard found a weak point between the two armies and many German troops were able to cross the *Autobahn* before the Soviet forces plugged the gap. The fighting was heavy and included continuous air attacks by the 2nd Air Army, as well as tree-bursting shells which rained wood splinters through the area. During the battle, the Soviet air force flew

2,459 attack missions and 1,683 bombing sorties.[347] The German forces found that they could not use their armour as well as they had hoped, because it was vulnerable to destruction on the roads and could not get a good grip on the sandy soil of the pine forests in the region. The German vanguard managed to reach and cross Reichsstrasse 96, south of Zossen and north of Baruth, where it was spotted by a Luftwaffe plane. Hitler was furious when he realised that Busse was attempting to break out west and not to come to his aid in Berlin. His command sent several messages demanding that the army turn towards Berlin, but received no answer.

During the night and the next day (April 27), the German forces renewed their attack along two axes south from the village of Halbe towards Baruth, and in the north from Teupitz. This attack failed to produce a mass breakout although, like the day before, some groups were able to slip through the Soviet lines.

The front lines were not continuous because the dense forest terrain meant that visibility was down to metres, so there was danger of ambush and sudden assault for both sides. Smoke from burning sections of the forest, set alight by shell fire, helped the Germans and hindered the Soviets because it shielded the Wehrmacht troops from aerial reconnaissance and attack. On the other hand, the smoke hindered many groups because, without a compass and no sun, it was difficult to judge which direction to go. The sandy soil precluded the digging of foxholes and there was no time to construct anything more elaborate, so there was little to no protection from wooden splinters created by artillery and tank HE shells, which the Soviet forces deliberately aimed to explode at tree-top height.

The third breakout attempt

On the night of April 28, the German forces tried another mass breakout from around Halbe. They broke through the 50th Guards Rifle Division and created a corridor from Halbe to the west, but paid a very high price. During April 28 and 29, the Soviets reinforced the flanks and attacked from the south, pouring in Katyusha rockets and shells, concentrating on the area around the Halbe.

By this time, the German troops were spread out over a wide area. The rearguard was at Storkow and the vanguard had linked up with the 12th Army at Beelitz. There were large groups around Halbe. The Soviet battle plan was to split the caterpillar into segments and then destroy each segment individually. The German battle plan was to continue moving west as fast as possible, keeping the corridor open.

The situation in Halbe was desperate for the Germans. Orders were still being issued to recognisable formations, but these were by now all mixed up. There was considerable tension between the Waffen-SS and Wehrmacht troops, with both accusing the other of helping their own while ignoring the plight of the other. In Halbe itself, some of the civilians took pity on very young soldiers ("*Kindersoldaten*") and allowed them to change out of their uniforms into civilian clothes. In one documented case, an SS man appeared at the door of a cellar intending to shoot a *Panzerfaust* into a cellar with about 40 civilians and young Wehrmacht soldiers in it, only to be shot dead by one of the soldiers.[347]

During the following days, the fighting became more and more confused. If the Germans came into contact with Soviet forces and overran a Soviet position, the Soviets counter-attacked not only with ground forces, but with artillery and aircraft. Losses on both sides were very high. By the time the fighting was over, (around the end of April, beginning of May), about 25,000 German soldiers had escaped to join up with the 12th Army on the eastern side of Reichsstrasse 2, the road running north-south through Beelitz.

Although this was the end of the Battle of Halbe, it was not the end of the breakout. Some 9th Army forces were again surrounded west of Luckenwalde by the north-westerly thrust of the 4th Guards Tank Army, only 10 km away from German 12th Army troops.Wikipedia:Citation needed The combined German 12th Army and 9th Army remnants then retreated westwards towards the Elbe so that they could surrender to American forces, which had halted their advance on the west bank of the river. The bulk of the fleeing German forces, along with several thousand civilians, reached and crossed the Elbe using the partially destroyed bridge at Tangermünde between 4 May and 7 May 1945, surrendering to elements of the U.S. 102nd Infantry Division, U.S. 9th Army, until Soviet forces reached the eastern bridgehead and halted further crossings.

Aftermath

The casualties on both sides were high. There are about 15,000 Germans buried in the cemetery at Halbe, making it the largest war cemetery in Germany from World War II. About 10,000 are unidentified soldiers killed during the first half of 1945.[348] The Red army claimed to have killed 60,000 German soldiers and taken 120,000 as prisoners. The number of prisoners is confirmed by German official sources,[349] while other sources consider it to be exaggerated.[348] Thousands of Red Army soldiers died trying to stop the breakout; most being buried at a cemetery next to the Baruth–Zossen road (Bundesstraße 96). These are the known dead, but the remains of more who died in the battle are found every year, so the total will never be known. Nobody knows how many civilians died, but it could have been as high as 10,000.[350]

> *The most astonishing part of the story is not the numbers who died or were forced to surrender but the 25,000 soldiers and several thousand civilians who succeeded in getting through three lines of Soviet troops.*

—*Antony Beevor*[350]

Formations involved in the battle

Soviet Union

Ground Forces[341]

- 1st Belorussian Front – Marshal G.K. Zhukov
  - 3rd Army – Colonel General A.V. Gorbatov
  - 69th Army – Colonel General V.Y. Kolpakchi
  - 33rd Army – Colonel General V.D. Svotaev
  - 2nd Guards Cavalry Corps – Lieutenant General V.V.Kruhkov
- 1st Ukrainian Front – Marshal I.S. Konev
  - 3rd Guards Army – Colonel General V.N.Gordov
  - 13th Army – Colonel General N.P.Phukhov
  - 28th Army – Lieutenant General A.A.Luchinsky
  - 3rd Guards Tank Army – Colonel General P.S. Rybalko
  - 4th Guards Tank Army – Colonel General D.D. Lelyushenko

Air Forces – Chief Marshal of Aviation A.A. Novikov

- 2nd Air Army – Colonel General Stepan Krasovsky
- 16th Air Army – Colonel General Sergei Rudenko
- 18th Air Army – Air Vice Marshal A.Y. Golovanov

Germany

- Ninth Army – General Theodor Busse
  - XI SS Panzer Corps – SS-General Matthias Kleinheisterkamp
  - V SS Mountain Corps – SS-General Friedrich Jeckeln
  - V Army Corps – General Dr. Ing. Kurt Wäger
- Army Support Troops
  - 21st Panzer Division
  - 10th SS Panzer Division "Frundsberg"
- Twelfth Army – General Walther Wenck
  - XX Corps – General Carl-Erik Koehler
  - XXXIX Panzer Corps – Lieutenant General Karl Arndt
  - XXXXI Panzer Corps – Lieutenant General Rudolf Holste
  - XXXXVIII Panzer Corps – General Maximilian von Edelsheim

References

Explanatory notes

Citations

Bibliography

- Beevor, Antony (2002). *Berlin: the Downfall, 1945*. Penguin Books. ISBN 978-0-670-88695-1.
- Le Tissier, Tony (2005). *Slaughter at Halbe*. Stroud: Sutton. ISBN 978-0-7509-3689-7.
- Ziemke, Earl Frederick (1969). *The Battle for Berlin: End of the Third Reich*. Ballantine; Macdonald. OCLC 59153427[351].
- Sennerteg, Niclas (2007). *Nionde Arméns Undergång: Kampen om Berlin 1945* (in Swedish). Lund: Historiska Media. ISBN 978-91-85507-43-6.

Further reading

- Luck, Hans von; *Panzer Commander – The Memoirs of Colonel Hans von Luck*; London: Cassell 2002, ISBN 978-0-304-36401-5.
- Ryan, Cornelius; *The Last Battle*; ISBN 978-0-684-80329-6
- Konev, I.S.; *Year of Victory*; ISBN 978-1-4102-1999-2.
- Remme, Tilman; The Battle for Berlin in World War II: Battle of Halbe[352] BBC website
- Ziemke Earl Frederick; *Stalingrad to Berlin. The German defeat in the east*; Honolulu, Hawaii : University Press of the Pacific, ©2003, ISBN 978-1-4102-0414-1.
- German defense minister honors Soviet dead in World War II[353]

Faust, Wolfgang: The Last Panther, Slaughter of the Reich, The breakout from the Halbe Kessel April-May 1945.A Panther Tank commander's personal memoir.(Bayern Classic Publications). Copyright; The Estate of Wolfgang Faust.

Appendix

References

[1] //tools.wmflabs.org/geohack/geohack.php?pagename=Battle_of_Berlin&params=52_31_N_13_23_E_region:DE-BE_type:event
[2] Zaloga 1982, p. 27.
[3] Glantz 1998, p. 261.
[4] Ziemke 1969, p. 71.
[5] Murray & Millett 2000, p. 482.
[6] Beevor 2002, p. 287.
[7] Antill 2005, p. 28.
[8] Glantz 1998, p. 373.
[9] Wagner 1974, p. 346.
[10] Bergstrom 2007, p. 117.
[11] Krivosheev 1997, p. 157.
[12] Krivosheev 1997, p. 263.
[13] Müller 2008, p. 673.
[14] Glantz 2001, p. 95.
[15] Antill 2005, p. 85.
[16] //en.wikipedia.org/w/index.php?title=Template:History_of_Berlin&action=edit
[17] Beevor 2002, pp. 400–405.
[18] Duffy 1991, pp. 24, 25.
[19] Hastings 2004, p. 295.
[20] Beevor 2002, p. 52.
[21] Duffy 1991, pp. 176–188.
[22] Duffy 1991, p. 293.
[23] Beevor 2002, p. 8.
[24] Tiemann 1998, p. 200.
[25] Beevor 2002, p. 9.
[26] Dollinger 1967, p. 198.
[27] Beevor 2002, p. 196.
[28] Williams 2005, p. 213.
[29] Bullock 1962, p. 753.
[30] Bullock 1962, pp. 778–781.
[31] Beevor 2002, p. 194.
[32] Williams 2005, pp. 310, 311.
[33] Ryan 1966, p. 135.
[34] Milward 1980, p. 303.
[35] McInnis 1946, p. 115.
[36] Beevor 2003, p. 219.
[37] Beevor 2002, Preface xxxiv, and pp. 138, 325.
[38] Beevor 2003, p. 166.
[39] Beevor 2003, p. 140.
[40] Williams 2005, p. 292.
[41] Zuljan 2003.
[42] Ziemke 1969, p. 76.
[43] Williams 2005, p. 293.
[44] Williams 2005, p. 322.
[45] Beevor 2003, p. 426.
[46] Gregory & Gehlen 2009, pp. 207–208.
[47] Beevor 2002, pp. 217–233.
[48] Hastings 2005, p. 468.
[49] Beevor 2002, p. 244.

[50] Beevor 2002, p. 247.
[51] Beevor 2003, p. 255.
[52] Beevor 2002, pp. 312–314.
[53] Ziemke 1969, p. 84.
[54] RAF staff 2006.
[55] Beevor 2002, pp. 255–256, 262.
[56] Beevor 2002, p. 337.
[57] Ziemke 1969, p. 88.
[58] Simons 1982, p. 78.
[59] Komorowski 2009, pp. 65–67.
[60] Beevor 2002, p. 345.
[61] Beevor 2003, p. 248.
[62] Beevor 2002, pp. 310–312.
[63] Ziemke 1969, pp. 87–88.
[64] Beevor 2002, p. 275.
[65] Ryan 1966, p. 436.
[66] Ziemke 1969, p. 89.
[67] Beevor 2003, p. 353.
[68] Ziemke 1969, p. 92.
[69] Lewis 1998, p. 465.
[70] states the appointment was on 23 April 1945; states "officially" it was the next morning of 24 April 1945; gives 26 April for Weidling's appointment.
[71] Ziemke 1969, pp. 92–94.
[72] Beevor 2002, p. 313.
[73] Ziemke 1969, p. 111.
[74] Fischer 2008, pp. 42–43.
[75] Beevor 2002, p. 223.
[76] Beevor 2002, p. 243.
[77] Ziemke 1969, p. 93.
[78] Beevor 2002, pp. 259, 297.
[79] Beevor 2002, pp. 291–292, 302.
[80] Beevor 2002, pp. 246–247.
[81] Beevor 2002, pp. 303–304.
[82] , states the centre sector was known as Z for Zentrum; , and , quoting General Mohnke directly refers to the smaller centre government quarter/district in this area and under his command as Z-Zitadelle.
[83] Beevor 2002, p. 340.
[84] Beevor 2002, pp. 257–258.
[85] Beevor 2003, pp. 371–373.
[86] Beevor 2002, p. 349.
[87] Beevor 2002, p. 343.
[88] Beevor 2003, p. 375.
[89] Beevor 2003, p. 377.
[90] Beevor 2003, p. 380.
[91] Hamilton 2008, p. 311.
[92] Beevor 2003, pp. 390–397.
[93] Sontheimer 2008.
[94] Bellamy 2007, pp. 663–7.
[95] Beevor 2002, p. 358.
[96] Bullock 1962, pp. 799, 800.
[97] Williams 2005, pp. 324, 325.
[98] Beevor 2003, p. 381.
[99] Beevor 2002, pp. 385–386.
[100] , states 3 am, and , 4 am, for Krebs' meeting with Chuikov
[101] Beevor 2003, p. 391.
[102] Dollinger 1967, p. 239.

[103] Beevor 2003, p. 405.
[104] Beevor 2003, p. 406.
[105] Beevor 2002, pp. 383–389.
[106] Ziemke 1969, pp. 125–126.
[107] Beevor 2002, p. 386.
[108] Beevor 2002, p. 391.
[109] Beevor 2002, p. 338.
[110] Dollinger 1967, p. 228.
[111] Ziemke 1969, p. 128.
[112] Ziemke 1969, p. 94.
[113] Ziemke 1969, p. 129.
[114] Beevor 2003, p. 350.
[115] Beevor 2003, pp. 345–346.
[116] Le Tissier 2005, p. 117.
[117] Le Tissier 2005, pp. 89, 90.
[118] Beevor 2002, p. 330.
[119] Ziemke 1969, p. 119.
[120] Ziemke 1969, p. 120.
[121] Beevor 2002, p. 350.
[122] Beevor 2002, p. 378.
[123] Beevor 2002, p. 395.
[124] Beevor 2002, p. 397.
[125] Krivosheev 1997, pp. 157,158.
[126] Krivosheev 1997, p. 3.
[127] Glantz 1998, p. 271.
[128] Clodfelter 2002, p. 515.
[129] Bellamy 2007, p. 670.
[130] White 2003, p. 126.
[131] Beevor 2002, p. 409.
[132] Beevor 2002, pp. 388–393.
[133] Bellamy 2007, pp. 660,670.
[134] Grossmann 2009, p. 51.
[135] Beevor 2002, pp. 326–327.
[136] Beevor & May 2002.
[137] Budnitskii 2015.
[138] Ziemke 1990, p. 303.
[139] Beevor 2002, p. 419.
[140] Ketchum 2014.
[141] rg.ru 2007.
[142] Kutylowski 2011.
[143] https://www.theguardian.com/g2/story/0,3604,707835,00.html
[144] https://web.archive.org/web/20081005071906/http://www.guardian.co.uk/g2/story/0%2C3604%2C707835%2C00.html
[145] https://web.archive.org/web/20150218155036/http://sti.clemson.edu/index.php?option=com_docman&task=doc_details&Itemid=310&gid=189
[146] http://sti.clemson.edu/index.php?option=com_docman&task=doc_details&gid=189&Itemid=310
[147] https://books.google.com/books?id=Qv3fJdwMQx0C&lpg=PP1&pg=PA207#v=onepage&q&f=false
[148] http://echo.msk.ru/programs/victory/697626-echo
[149] http://www.privateletters.net/medals_ussr.html
[150] https://books.google.com/books?id=XX5KcTNWbooC&pg=PA65
[151] http://www.polishtoledo.com/polishholidays.htm
[152] https://web.archive.org/web/20120728094923/http://www.raf.mod.uk/bombercommand/apr45.html
[153] http://www.raf.mod.uk/bombercommand/apr45.html

[154] http://www.rg.ru/2007/05/08/znamya.html

[155] https://web.archive.org/web/20110519173438/http://www.rg.ru/2007/05/08/znamya.html

[156] http://www.spiegel.de/international/europe/0,1518,551972,00.html

[157] https://web.archive.org/web/20080913155744/http://www.spiegel.de/international/europe/0%2C1518%2C551972%2C00.html

[158] http://www.history.army.mil/books/wwii/Occ-GY/ch17.htm

[159] http://www.globalsecurity.org/military/library/report/other/us-army_germany_1944-46_index.htm#contents

[160] //doi.org/10.1017/S0008938900001266

[161] https://web.archive.org/web/20110525014346/http://www.onwar.com/articles/9905.htm

[162] http://www.onwar.com/articles/9905.htm

[163] https://web.archive.org/web/20110514001340/http://www.onwar.com/faq.htm

[164] http://www.historyofwar.org/articles/battles_berlin.html

[165] https://web.archive.org/web/20071014200626/http://www.geocities.com/isanders_2000/ww2index.htm

[166] http://www.geocities.com/isanders_2000/ww2index.htm

[167] http://www.bbc.co.uk/history/worldwars/wwtwo/berlin_01.shtml

[168] https://web.archive.org/web/20070318230858/http://www.argo.net.au/andre/osmarwhiteENFIN.htm

[169] http://www.argo.net.au/andre/osmarwhiteENFIN.htm

[170] https://www.youtube.com/watch?v=wjD6Lxiu6q4

[171] http://niehorster.org/012_ussr/45-04-03_Berlin/_Front_2-Byelorussian.html

[172] http://niehorster.org/012_ussr/45-04-03_Berlin/_Front_1-Byelorussian.html

[173] http://niehorster.org/012_ussr/45-04-03_Berlin/_Front_1-Ukrainian.html

[174] //tools.wmflabs.org/geohack/geohack.php?pagename=Battle_of_the_Oder%E2%80%93Neisse&params=52_31_47.3_N_14_25_33.9_E_region:DE-BB_type:event

[175] Undoubtedly use of artillery was made throughout the operation, but initial bombardment rarely lasted longer than 2 hours, see pp.148–149, *Soviet military operational art: in pursuit of deep battle,* (1991)

[176] Beevor see References page 217

[177] Ziemke see References page 81

[178] Beevor see references page 217-233

[179] Ziemke see references page 82

[180] Ziemke see references page 83

[181] Ziemke see references page 92

[182]

[183] Ziemke see references page 94

[184]

[185] World War II Axis Military History Day-by-Day: April http://www.feldgrau.com/april.html 20 April 1945

[186] //tools.wmflabs.org/geohack/geohack.php?pagename=Battle_in_Berlin&params=52_31_7_N_13_22_34_E_region:DE-BE_type:event

[187] For the 45,000 soldiers and 40,000 *Volkssturm*. A large number of the 45,000 were troops of the LVI Panzer Corps that were at the start of the battle part of the German IX Army on the Seelow Heights .

[188] Beevor 2002, p. 287.

[189] Antill 2005, p. 85.

[190] Kiederling 1987, pp. 38–40.

[191] Beevor 2002, pp. 217–233.

[192] Ziemke 1969, p. 84.

[193] World War II Axis Military History Day-by-Day: April http://www.feldgrau.com/april.html 20 April 1945

[194] Beevor 2002, pp. 255–256, 262.

[195] Antony Beevor, speaking as himself in a television documentary: "Revealed" Hitler's Secret Bunkers https://www.imdb.com/title/tt1262365/, directed by George Pagliero (2008)

[196] Ziemke 1969, pp. 92–94.

[197] Ziemke 1969, p. 94.
[198] Ziemke 1969, p. 111.
[199] Fischer 2008, p. 42.
[200] Fischer 2008, pp. 42–43.
[201] The Soviets later estimated the number as 180,000, but this figure was calculated from the number of prisoners that they took and included many unarmed men in uniform, such as railway officials and members of the Reich Labour Service .
[202] Beevor 2002, p. 317.
[203] Prakash & Kruse 2008, pp. 44–46.
[204] "A Prussian law of 1875, enacted to cover the streets of Berlin, prescribed that the main avenues should be 95 feet or more in width, secondary thoroughfares from 65 to 95 feet and the local streets from 40 to 65 feet."
[205] "The Berlin streets are for the most part very broad and straight. They are surprisingly even; there is not a hill worthy of the name in the whole of the city" .
[206] "The highest hill in the ridge was the Kreuzberg, which stood at . It became the site of a Schinkel-designed monument erected in 1821 and gave its name to the most famous of Berlin's districts" .
[207] Ladd 1998, pp. 99–102.
[208] Beevor 2002, pp. 316–319.
[209] Beevor 2012, p. 565.
[210] , states the appointment was 23 April; , states "officially" it was the next morning of 24 April; , gives 26 April for Weidling's appointment.
[211] Beevor 2002, pp. 259, 297.
[212] Beevor 2002, p. 297.
[213] Beevor 2002, pp. 291–292.
[214] Beevor 2002, pp. 291–292, 302–304.
[215] Beevor states the centre sector was known as Z for Zentrum ; while Fischer and Tiemann, quoting General Mohnke directly refers to the smaller centre government quarter/district in this area and under his command as Z-Zitadelle (*"Citadel"*) (, and).
[216] Beevor 2002, p. 303.
[217] Ziemke 1969, pp. 114–115.
[218] Beevor 2002, pp. 303–304, 319.
[219] Tiemann 1998, pp. 339, 340.
[220] Dollinger 1997, p. 228.
[221] Beevor 2002, p. 322.
[222] Ziemke 1969, p. 98.
[223] Tiemann 1998, p. 339.
[224] Beevor 2002, p. 321.
[225] Beevor 2002, pp. 318–320.
[226] Beevor 2002, pp. 323–324, 17, 318.
[227]
[228] Beevor 2002, pp. 319–320.
[229] Beevor 2002, p. 323.
[230] Ziemke 1969, p. 119.
[231] Kershaw 2008, pp. 943–947.
[232] Ziemke 1969, p. 118.
[233] Antony Beevor writes that the incident is contentious and that the number of dead and the day of the incident vary. He states that orders were given by Krukenberg to a group of *Nordland* sappers on 1 May (after Hitler's death) and that the charge probably did not go off until the early hours of 2 May . Stephan Hamilton finds it more likely that the tunnel system "flooded due to several broken locks caused by the thousands of tons of heavy Soviet artillery and rocket fire". He points out that it would not make any sense for the SS to flood the tunnels when "The U-Bahn tunnel system in Berlin's centre served key functions for the defenders like command-and-control centers, makeshift hospitals and supply points. In addition, the Germans effectively used the system to move quickly around the city to attack the Russians. Even the SS maintained

several combat HQs along the *U-Bahn* line that ran north-south from the *Stadtmitte U-Bahn* station" .

[234] Beevor 2002, p. 351.

[235] Beevor 2002, p. 340.

[236] Map of the Battle for Reichstag 29 April – 2 May 1945 http://www.onwar.com/maps/wwii/ eastfront2/reichstag45.htm . This map is copied from , *Battle For Berlin: End Of The Third Reich*

[237] Beevor 2002, pp. 340, 347–349.

[238] The Luftwaffe order differs in different sources. Beevor states it was to attack Potsdamerplatz , but Ziemke asserts it was to support Wenck's XII Army attack . Both agree that he was also ordered to make sure Himmler was punished.

[239] Beevor 2002, p. 342.

[240] Dollinger 1997, p. 239.

[241] Beevor 2002, p. 343.

[242] On the MI5 website, using sources available to Hugh Trevor-Roper (a Second World War MI5 agent and historian/author of *The Last Days of Hitler*), records the marriage as taking place **after** Hitler had dictated his last will and testament .

[243] Beevor 2002, p. 338.

[244] Exton, Brett. *Some of the prisoners held at Special Camp 11: Generaloberst Gotthard Heinrici http://www.islandfarm.fsnet.co.uk/Generaloberst%20Gotthard%20Heinrici.htm*

[245] Exton, Brett, and Murphy, Richard. Some of the prisoners held at Special Camp 11: General der Infanterie Kurt von Tippelskirch http://www.bridgend-powcamp.fsnet.co.uk/General% 20der%20Infanterie%20Kurt%20von%20Tippelskirch.htm

[246] Ziemke 1969, p. 128.

[247] Beevor 2002, p. 349.

[248] Beevor 2002, pp. 352–353.

[249] Beevor 2002, p. 352.

[250] Ziemke 1969, p. 120.

[251] last paragraph

[252] , says Jodl replied, but , and , say it was Keitel

[253] Le Tissier 2010, p. 29.

[254] Komornicki 1967, p. 146.

[255] Le Tissier 2010, p. 173.

[256] Komornicki 1967, pp. 220–221.

[257] Komornicki 1967, p. 151.

[258] Zbiniewicz 1988, p. 272.

[259] Komornicki 1967, p. 170.

[260] Komornicki 1967, p. 174.

[261] Komornicki 1967, p. 178.

[262] Komornicki 1967, p. 181.

[263] Beevor 2002, pp. 354–355.

[264] , for the size of the AAA

[265] Beevor 2002, pp. 356–357.

[266] Beevor 2002, p. 358.

[267] Joachimsthaler 1999, pp. 160–182.

[268] Kershaw 2008, p. 955.

[269] Kershaw 2008, p. 954.

[270] Komornicki 1967, pp. 182–184.

[271] Komornicki 1967, pp. 190–197.

[272] Beevor 2002, pp. 365–367, 372.

[273] Hamilton 2008, p. 311.

[274] Hamilton 2008, p. 312.

[275] Komornicki 1967, pp. 200–209.

[276] Hamilton 2008, pp. 312–313.

[277] Komornicki 1967, pp. 212–219.

[278] Komornicki 1967, pp. 224–229.

[279] Komornicki 1967, p. 232.
[280] , states 3am, and , 4am, for Krebs meeting with Chuikov
[281] Beevor 2002, pp. 380–381.
[282] Beevor 2002, pp. 372–375.
[283] , says that Weidling gave no orders for a breakout.
[284] Beevor 2002, p. 382.
[285] Weidendammer Brücke de.wikipedia.org
[286] Beevor 2002, pp. 383, 389.
[287] Le Tissier 2010, p. 188.
[288] Beevor 2002, p. 383.
[289] Ziemke 1969, p. 125.
[290] Beevor 2002, p. 384.
[291] Beevor 2002, pp. 384, 385.
[292] Beevor 2002, pp. 388–389.
[293] Beevor 2002, pp. 384, 385, 388.
[294] Beevor 2002, p. 388.
[295] Beevor 2002, p. 386.
[296] Beevor 2002, pp. 287, 388–393.
[297] Beevor 2002, p. 409.
[298] Beevor, Antony; "They raped every German female from eight to 80" https://www.theguardian.com/g2/story/0,3604,707835,00.html 1 May, The Guardian, 2002
[299] https://books.google.com/books?id=vAzgsCDUky0C&printsec=frontcover#v=onepage&q&f=false
[300] https://books.google.com/books?id=McFVHAAACAAJ
[301] //www.worldcat.org/oclc/5297730
[302] https://books.google.com/books?id=T4RDOfb3XgQC&pg=PA99&redir_esc=y#v=onepage&q&f=false
[303] https://www.mi5.gov.uk/home/about-us/who-we-are/mi5-history/world-war-ii/hitlers-last-days.html
[304] https://books.google.com/books?id=rDGd7HDMFp4C&pg=PA44
[305] https://books.google.com/books?id=j4gTGOMAOyEC&pg=PA7#v=onepage&q&f=false
[306] http://www.historyofwar.org/articles/battles_berlin.html#app1
[307] http://www.historyofwar.org/articles/battles_berlin.html#app2
[308] http://www.bbc.co.uk/history/worldwars/wwtwo/berlin_01.shtml
[309] https://www.webcitation.org/5knwb8rds?url=http://www.geocities.com/isanders_2000/ww2index.htm
[310] http://www.geocities.com/isanders_2000/ww2index.htm
[311] //doi.org/10.2307/120398
[312] https://web.archive.org/web/20070318230858/http://www.argo.net.au/andre/osmarwhiteENFIN.htm
[313] http://www.argo.net.au/andre/osmarwhiteENFIN.htm
[314] Dallas 2006, p. 3.
[315] Tissier 1999, p. 168.
[316] Lucas 2010.
[317] Beevor 2003, pp. 390–397.
[318] Sontheimer 2008.
[319] Griffin, Michael (199). "The Great War Photographs: Constructing Myths of History and Photojournalism". In Bonnie Brennen & Hanno Hardt eds., Picturing the Past: Media, History & Photography. (pp. 122–157). Urbana: University of Illinois Press. p. 144.
[320] Tissier 1999, p. 124.
[321] Antill & Dennis 2005, p. 76.
[322] Adams 2008, p. 48.
[323] Broekmeyer 2004, p. 130.
[324] Walkowitz & Knauer 2004, p. 83.
[325]
[326]

[327] http://www.spiegel.de/netzwelt/gadgets/0,1518,667710,00.html

[328] http://www.famouspictures.org/flag-on-the-reichstag/

[329] http://www.spiegel.de/international/europe/0,1518,551972,00.html

[330] http://www.mk.ru/regions/nijniy-novgorod/article/2010/05/12/486114-za-nego-gering-poluchil-po-shee.html

[331] https://www.usatoday.com/news/world/2008-06-15-2109452_x.htm

[332] https://www.usatoday.com/news/world/2008-06-16-WWII-photo_N.htm

[333] http://diario.latercera.com/2010/02/18/01/contenido/8_24322_9.html

[334] https://www.theguardian.com/world/2010/feb/17/soldier-reichstag-photo-dies

[335] //tools.wmflabs.org/geohack/geohack.php?pagename=Battle_of_Halbe&params=52_6_24_N_13_42_3_E_type:event

[336] Le Tissier 2005, p. 206.

[337] Ziemke 1969, pp. 476–477.

[338] Beevor 2002, p. 330.

[339] Beevor 2002, p. 329.

[340] Le Tissier 2005, p. 81.

[341] Le Tissier 2005, Appendices.

[342] Le Tissier 2005, p. 83, Disposition Map of 25 April.

[343] Le Tissier 2005, p. 89–90.

[344] Le Tissier 2005, p. 117–119.

[345] Le Tissier 2005, pp. 91–92.

[346] Le Tissier 2005, p. 84–88.

[347] Beevor 2002, p. 334.

[348] Sennerteg 2007, p. 378.

[349] Brandenburgische Landeszentrale für politische Bildung:Die Kesselschlacht http://www.politische-bildung-brandenburg.de/themen/rechtsextremismus/dagegen/denkort-halbe/die-kesselschlacht

[350] Beevor 2002, p. 337.

[351] //www.worldcat.org/oclc/59153427

[352] http://www.bbc.co.uk/history/worldwars/wwtwo/berlin_04.shtml

[353] http://en.ce.cn/World/Europe/200505/01/t20050501_3747692.shtml

Article Sources and Contributors

The sources listed for each article provide more detailed licensing information including the copyright status, the copyright owner, and the license conditions.

Battle of Berlin *Source:* https://en.wikipedia.org/w/index.php?oldid=853166586 *License:* Creative Commons Attribution-Share Alike 3.0 *Contributors:* AlejandroR1990, Alex Shih, Anomalocaris, Anotherclown, Antifa38, Ar2678, Archsouls, Arkar1984, Armenius vambery, Assassin3577, BD2412, Bender235, Binksternet, Brechindunc, Brigade Piron, Buckshot06, Bulls123, Capt Jim, CarlGGHamilton, Carlotm, Chiswick Chap, Choy4311, ClueBot NG, CocstanzKWGO, CombatWombat42, CommonsDelinker, CurtisNaito, Cyberbot II, DMorpheus2, Darthkenobi0, Denniss, Diannaa, Dissident93, Drumandtamaya1, El C, Elockid, EmreErguder, Ericoides, Ernio48, Excirial, Faceless Enemy, Favonian, Fixer88, Flowerpotman, Flyer22 Reborn, Frangars, Gap9551, Garchy, GeneralizationsAreBad, Gerrit, Gjs238, Gog the Mild, Grngu, Gunbirddriver, Hammersoft, Helenabella, Heron, Hohum, I need a name, ImperatorPublius, Iryna Harpy, Italia2006, J 1982, JSquish, Jackfork, Jdaloner, JoeSperrazza, John, Joshualouie711, Jroehl, Jtgelt, K.e.coffman, Kablammo, Kges1901, Kierzek, KoopaTroopa, Layla, the remover, Laytar1, LightandDark2000, LittleJerry, Look2See1, Lovkal, Lucasjohansson, MRD2014, Magioladitis, Marek69, MartinKassemJ120, Maxaxax, MisterBee1966, Mohawk.85, MusikAnimal, My very best wishes, Nick-D, OnBeyondZebrux, Owain Knight, PBS, Paavo273, Parkwells, PeerBaba, Piledhigheranddeeper, Pranith, Quondum, RJANKA, Rcbutcher, Rrburke, Rrostrom, Sd31263, Shellwood, ShockD, Siberian Husky, SkonesMickLoud, Skybunny, Slightsmile, Somakip, Spinningsparks, Spyglasses, Staberinde, StuRat, Sundostund, Superlynx98, Surv1v4l1st, TeckHawk, The Madras, The PIPE, The Pittsburgher, The Rambling Man, Thqldpxm, Tim!, Tiptoety, Tom5551, Trappist the monk, TwinkleMore, UNSC Luke 1021, Valetude, Vincinio, Volunteer Marek, Widgetdog, Widr, Witchchester, Wotvietnam, Wroclaw2468, YMB29, Yoloswaggerswag, Zawed, ÁDA - DÁP, Илья Драконов, 100 anonymous edits 1

Order of battle for the Battle of Berlin *Source:* https://en.wikipedia.org/w/index.php?oldid=839371131 *License:* Creative Commons Attribution-Share Alike 3.0 *Contributors:* BD2412, BruceLevesque, Cornellrockey, Corpusfury, Hamish59, JMRAMOS0109, Jonesey95, Kges1901, MisterBee1966, Onel5969, PBS, Peacemaker67, Ryan.opel, ScreiberBike, Slon02, Vermont, Wargo, Welsh, 6 anonymous edits 27

Battle of the Oder–Neisse *Source:* https://en.wikipedia.org/w/index.php?oldid=854032301 *License:* Creative Commons Attribution-Share Alike 3.0 *Contributors:* 994224004j, Akhil999in, Alexdan loghin, Altenmann, Altmany, Athenaeum, Buckshot06, Caerwine, ChrisGualtieri, Cyfal, Cyrosept, Davecrosby uk, David J Johnson, Davidcannon, DavisGL, Dimadick, Dodo19~enwiki, GoShow, Gobonobo, Grafikm fr, Hamish59, HanzoHattori, Italia2006, Jake V, Jaraalbe, Jdaloner, Juan Gabriel Simois, K.e.coffman, Kevinsam, Kirill Lokshin, Kwamikagami, LanternLight, Leebo, LilHelpa, Los688, M3ZZ', Magnet For Knowledge, Marcocapelle, Mrg3105, NuclearWarfare, Ohconfucius, Olessi, PBS, Piotrus, Rjwilmsi, Roger Davies, Rshu, Ryan.opel, Simbagraphix, Skyerise, The Anomebot2, Tim!, Tom.Reding, TwinkleMore, Valentinian, Woohookitty, 26 anonymous edits 37

Battle in Berlin *Source:* https://en.wikipedia.org/w/index.php?oldid=848335631 *License:* Creative Commons Attribution-Share Alike 3.0 *Contributors:* 2001:db8, ABritinCan, Alansohn, Altenmann, Andrwsc, Anthony Appleyard, Audaciter, Aymatth2, B14709, BD2412, Backpackadam, Bahavd Gita, Bcaulf, Berean Hunter, BokicaK, Br'er Rabbit, Brigade Piron, Buster7, Candido, ChrisGualtieri, Chumchum7, ClueBot NG, CommonsDelinker, Corpusfury, Cyfal, DadaNeem, DagosNavy, Dcirovic, De728631, Deathlibrarian, Diannaa, Dissident93, Di2000, DocYako, Dodo19~enwiki, DrFrench, FJS15, Fixer88, Frietjes, Fury 1991, Gabbeman1, Gaius Cornelius, Gareth Griffith-Jones, Gilliam, Gob Lofa, GoingBatty, Hamish59, Hmains, Illegitimate Barrister, Italia2006, Jack Merridew, Jd2718, Jdaloner, John of Reading, K.e.coffman, KConWiki, Kevinsam, Kierzek, Kithira, Klemen Kocjancic, LanternLight, Lemnaminor, Magioladitis, MartinKassemJ120, Mauls, Maxl, Metalhead94, Mhardcastle, MisterBee1966, Mowerbyte, MyMoloboaccount, Natg 19, Niceguyedc, Nick Number, Nick-D, Niremetal, Ohconfucius, PBS, Piotrus, Quentin X, RASAM, Rcbutcher, Reenem, Remotelysensed, Rexagu2, Rich Farmbrough, Rjwilmsi, Robert1947, Salociin, Skybunny, Soenke Rahn, Starbois, Sundostund, Tabletop, The Anomebot2, TheFreeWorld, TheRealSingapore, Tim!, Ulf Heinsohn, Valenciano, Valoem, Vanished user uih38riiw4hjlsd, WOSlinker, Whoop whoop pull up, Wikih101, Woohookitty, Yopie, Zawed, 116 anonymous edits 43

Raising a Flag over the Reichstag *Source:* https://en.wikipedia.org/w/index.php?oldid=853240843 *License:* Creative Commons Attribution-Share Alike 3.0 *Contributors:* 4567L, 72, 8digits, Adel.M.Radwan, Arminden, Asimov123, Bbb23, Bellerophon5685, Brandmeister, CWenger, Calidum, De728631, Deltabeignet, Deor, Dexos, Donner60, Dratman, Drmies, El Grafo, EoGuy, Esemono, Farrus Octara, Funandtrvl, GeoRugby, George Serdechny, Glane23, Good Olfactory, Grover cleveland, Grubberry, Gutc2003, Heroeswithmetaphors, Hmains, Hohum, Ibadibam, Idknicci, Igel 14, Inateadaze, Iseult, JMS Old Al, John of Reading, JustAGal, Jwillbur, K.e.coffman, Kierzek, Klemen Kocjancic, Koavf, KylieTastic, L.Safranek, LanternLight, Manushand, Maschen, Mckinley99, Metalllinux, Mikhail Ryazanov, Monochrome Monitor, Moscow Connection, MtulliusC, Nanami Kamimura, NiTenIchiRyu, Nick Number, Nwbeeson, Opencooper, P. S. Burton, PBS, Pharos, Piledhigheranddeeper, Pincrete, Polentarion, Primaler, RASAM, RabitsVinge, Redalert2fan, RevelationDirect, Richard Arthur Norton (1958-), Sammimack, SchreiberBike, Sfan00 IMG, Sheila1988, Skittles the hog, Someone not using his real name, Sourenaaa, Sturmgeewhr88, Superwont, Syko, Tbhotch, TeaOhEm, The Anome, The Anomebot2, The PIPE, Tim!, Timrollpickering, Toddy1, UCaetano, Udibi, Utahcox, Vitriden, Whywhenwhohow, YSSYguy, Yintan, А. Погодин, 91 anonymous edits 69

Battle of Halbe *Source:* https://en.wikipedia.org/w/index.php?oldid=854032880 *License:* Creative Commons Attribution-Share Alike 3.0 *Contributors:* Adel.M.Radwan, Adumoul, Adûnâi, Altenmann, Andreas1968, Angilbas, Asmaybe, Auntof6, BD2412, BOT-Superzerocool, Bad Night, Bahavd Gita, Banksmeister general, Bbartlog, BernardZ, Bernd.Brincken, Bleakcomb, Bob O'Bob, Bobo192, Bryan Derksen, Buchbibliothek, Buckshot06, Buster-1968, Clarityfiend, Cyfal, CylonCAG, Dabbler, Darkwind, Dead Mary, Deb, Denniss, Dewritech, DocYako, Dodo19~enwiki, Dvavasour, Eggishorn, EncMstr, EriFr, Everyking, EyeTruth, FishHeadAbcd, G-41614, Gaius Cornelius, Gaius Octavius Princeps, Gbinal, Hamish59, HanzoHattori, Hirsch.im.wald, Hmains, Huon, Ibericus Lusitanus, JamesAM, Jan Hoellwarth, Jaraalbe, Jd2718, Jdaloner, Jeagerca, Jim Sweeney, Jj137, Jmorrison230582, John of Reading, Jpotts, Jtgelt, K.e.coffman, Klex79~enwiki, Kesron, Kubanczyk, Kurt Leyman, LanternLight, Laytar1, Loopy, Mads Lange, Malayedit, Marcocapelle, MarshallPoe, Meeepmep, Michael.Kramer, MisterBee1966, Mkpumphrey, Modulatum, Monk, Mrg3105, Mztourist, Niceguyedc, Oberiko, Olessi, PBS, PMLawrence, Pearle, Pluke, PocciiScript, Reenem, Rjwilmsi, RobShaz, Robert1947, Roger Davies, Rroww, Rune.welsh, Ryan.opel, SS451, Sam Hocevar, Savar, Sheehan, Sledge139, Socrates2008, StarSword, SuperDeng, TAMilo, Terrasidius, TheCheeseManCan, ThreeBlindMice, Tim!, Tswold@msn.com, TwinkleMore, Undoctor, Utanov66, Varlaam, Volker89, Wanderer602, WereSpielChequers, Whoop whoop pull up, World war 2 expert, Wreck Smurfy, Wwoods, Yoyoyoma, Кашак, 110 anonymous edits 75

Image Sources, Licenses and Contributors

The sources listed for each image provide more detailed licensing information including the copyright status, the copyright owner, and the license conditions.

License

Index

www.ingramcontent.com/pod-product-compliance
Lightning Source LLC
Chambersburg PA
CBHW031537040426
42445CB00010B/580